CW01338298

The Imitation of Christ

A Pre-teen's Guide to Awesomeness

Thomas Kempis
Lukasz Dziewiecki

Contents

PREFACE: Epic Heroes Who Loved This Book! 7

Chapter 1: Following Jesus: The Ultimate Squad Leader! 9

Chapter 2: The Ultimate Guide to Not Being a Show-Off! 12

Chapter 3: Truth-Seeker Mode: ACTIVATED! 16

Chapter 4: The Ultimate Guide to Not Being a Total Noob at Life Decisions! 20

Chapter 5: How to Level Up Your Bible Reading Game! 24

Chapter 6: How to Stop Being a Slave to Your Likes and Wants! 27

Chapter 7: How to Drop the Ego and Level Up Your Humility! .. 30

Chapter 8: The Ultimate Guide to Not Being BFFs with EVERYONE! 33

Chapter 9: The Epic Guide to Being a Good Team Player! 36

Chapter 10: How to Not Be That Kid Who Never Shuts Up! 39

Chapter 11: How to Level Up Your Inner Peace Game! 43

Chapter 12: How to Level Up Through Life's Hard Stuff! 46

Chapter 13: Temptation Takedown: Your Guide to Not Getting Played! 49

Chapter 14: How to Not Be That Kid Who Judges Everyone! 52

Chapter 15: The Epic Guide to Being a Real-Life Hero! 56

Chapter 16: How to Deal With People Who Drive You Crazy! ... 60

Chapter 17: So You Think Being Religious Makes You Boring? WRONG! 63

Chapter 18: Learning from the OG Saints (Without Falling Asleep!) 65

Chapter 19: The Not-So-Boring Guide to Being a Spiritual Champion! 68

Chapter 20: The Ultimate Guide to Finding Peace When Life Is CRAZY! 71

Chapter 21: The Heart Check: When Your Feelings Feel Like a Roller Coaster! 74

Chapter 22: The Ultimate Guide to Handling Life's Epic Fails! ... 77

Chapter 23: The Not-So-Fun Guide to Thinking About Death (But We'll Make It Interesting!) 80

Chapter 24: The Epic Guide to Not Freaking Out About Judgment Day! 83

Chapter 25: The Epic Makeover Guide: How to Level Up Your ENTIRE Life! 86

Chapter 26: How to Level Up Your Prayer Game (Without Falling Asleep!) 89

Chapter 27: How to Stop Being Obsessed with Yourself (Without Having an Identity Crisis!) 92

Chapter 28: How to Handle Haters (Without Becoming One Yourself!) 95

Chapter 29: How to Stay Cool When Life Feels Like a Dumpster Fire! 98

Chapter 30: How to Get God's Help Without Looking Desperate! 101

Chapter 31: How to Focus on God When Everything's Distracting! 104

Chapter 33: How to Keep Your Heart On Track When It's Acting Like a GPS Having a Breakdown! 109

Chapter 34: How to Actually Love God When Netflix Exists! ... 112

The "Making God More Interesting Than Your Phone" Challenge 112

Chapter 35: How to Handle Temptation When Everything Looks Like a Cookie! 115

3

Chapter 37: How to Give Up Your Ego Without Becoming a Doormat! 120

Chapter 38: How to Let God Be Your Life's Project Manager (Without Micromanaging Him Back!) 122

Chapter 39: How to Stay Focused When Your Brain Has 47 Browser Tabs Open! 125

Chapter 40: How to Stop Being Your Own Worst Critic (Without Becoming Your Biggest Fan!) 128

Chapter 41: How to Not Care About Fame When Everyone's Chasing Clout! 131

Chapter 42: How to Not Base Your Happiness on Other People's Moods! 133

Chapter 43: How to Not Be a Know-It-All While Actually Knowing Stuff! 136

Chapter 44: How to Not Stress About Everything When The World's Gone Crazy! 138

Chapter 45: How to Not Believe Everything You Hear (Without Becoming a Total Skeptic)! 141

Chapter 46: How to Handle Haters Without Becoming One! ..144

Chapter 47: How to Boss Life When Life is Being a Boss! 147

Chapter 48: How to Think About Eternity Without Having an Existential Crisis! 150

Chapter 49: How to Be Hyped for Heaven Without Checking Out Early! 153

Chapter 50: How to Hand Your Mess to God Without Dropping Your Pizza! 156

Chapter 51: How to Do Small Things Without Feeling Like a Small Fry! 159

Chapter 52: How to Stay Humble Without Becoming a Human Doormat! 161

4

Chapter 53: How to Stay Spiritual When Everything's Screaming "MATERIAL GIRL!"..164

Chapter 55: How to Level Up Your Spirit When Your Human Side is Being Sus!..169

Chapter 56: How to Follow Jesus Without Becoming Weird About It!..172

Chapter 57: How to Bounce Back When You've Face-Planted in Life!...174

Chapter 58: How to Trust God When Life Makes Zero Sense! 177

Chapter 59: How to Make God Your Ultimate Support System Without Being Clingy!...179

Book 4, Chapter 1: How to Meet Jesus Without Fainting!.......182

The "Meeting the Ultimate VIP" Guide....................................182

Book 4, Chapter 2: God's Ultimate Plot Twist - The Greatest Love Story Ever!..185

The "God's Love is Way Bigger Than Your Phone's Storage" Guide 185

Book 4, Chapter 3: Why Frequent Communion is Better Than Your Social Media Feed!..188

The "More Jesus, Less Drama" Guide 188

Book 4, Chapter 4: The Ultimate Power-Up: Holy Communion's Epic Bonus Pack!...192

The "Better Than Any Legendary Drop" Guide.........................192

Book 4, Chapter 5: Why Being a Priest is More Epic Than Being a Superhero!...195

The "Ultimate Sacred Power" Guide...195

Book 4, Chapter 6: How to Get Ready for Holy Communion Without Having a Spiritual Panic Attack!...................................199

The "Divine Meet-Up Prep" Guide...199

Book 4, Chapter 7: The Ultimate Soul Spring Cleaning Guide! 203

The "Checking Your Spiritual Closet" Manual 203

Book 4, Chapter 8: The Great Trade Deal: Giving Up Everything for Everything! 206

Introduction: The Ultimate Exchange Program 206

Book 4, Chapter 9: How to Be God's Gift To Everyone (The Right Way!) 210

MISSION BRIEFING: Operation Total Gift Mode 210

Book 4, Chapter 10: Why Skipping Communion is Like Missing Out on Free Legendary Loot! 214

DOWNLOADING DIVINE WISDOM... 214

Book 4, Chapter 11: The Ultimate Power Duo: Jesus and the Bible! 218

Book 4, Chapter 12: Getting Ready to Meet Jesus: The Ultimate Pre-Game Guide! 222

PREFACE: Epic Heroes Who Loved This Book!

Hey there! Before you dive into this book, you need to know something amazing: some of the most incredible heroes in history kept this book as their personal power-up guide!

The Man Who Sneaked Into a Death Camp 🕵️‍♂️

Ever heard of Witold Pilecki? This guy was like a real-life superhero who did something absolutely mind-blowing: he CHOSE to go into one of the worst Nazi death camps (Auschwitz) as a prisoner! Why? Because he wanted to tell the world about the horrible things happening there and organize a resistance from inside.

Think about that for a second - while most of us complain about having to clean our rooms, this guy voluntarily walked into what was basically hell on Earth to help others!

Before his death (yeah, sadly the bad guys got him in the end), he told his wife to make sure their kids read two books: the Bible and "The Imitation of Christ." He knew these books had the cheat codes his children would need to level up in life and become truly strong people.

Other Epic Heroes Who Loved This Book 📖

- Thomas More: This guy was so brave he faced execution (like, actual execution!) with a smile, and he kept this book with him right up until the end.
- Dietrich Bonhoeffer: Imagine living in Nazi Germany and standing up to Hitler himself! That's what this hero did, and guess what book helped him stay brave?
- Soldiers in World War I: These guys carried small copies of this book in their pockets while fighting in muddy trenches and dodging bullets!

Why This Book is Different 🎮

Now, you might be thinking, "Great, another boring old book." NOPE! We've totally transformed it into something you can actually understand and enjoy. We've:

- Replaced all the old-timey language with words you actually use

- Added fun examples that make sense in your world
- Threw in some humor (because being good doesn't mean being boring)
- Included gaming references (because life is kind of like a video game with eternal consequences)

What's In It For You? ♂

This book is like having a cheat code for:
- Dealing with bullies
- Handling tough times
- Making good choices
- Becoming stronger on the inside
- Leveling up your character stats

The Bottom Line 🐟

If some of the bravest people in history found this book helpful enough to recommend it with their literal dying breath, imagine what it could do for you!

Remember: Heroes aren't just people who do big things - they're people who do the right things, even when it's hard. This book has been helping people become heroes for over 500 years.

Ready to start your hero's journey? Let's dive in!

P.S. - Don't worry, we've made sure this version won't put you to sleep. Promise! ☺

[Now onto Chapter 1, where your adventure begins...]

Note: We kept all the wisdom but made it as exciting as your favorite video game. Because being good doesn't have to be boring!

Chapter 1: Following Jesus: The Ultimate Squad Leader!

Yo dudes! Ever wondered what it would be like to join the most epic squad ever? Well, buckle up because we're about to talk about following the ultimate squad leader - Jesus Christ! 🎮

The No-Darkness Challenge

You know how in video games you sometimes need a torch or night-vision goggles to see in dark places? Jesus once dropped this absolute gem: "Anyone who follows me won't be walking around in the dark!" Think of Jesus as your spiritual night-vision goggles! Pretty cool, right?

But here's the thing - this isn't just about hitting the "follow" button like on social media. It's about actually trying to live like Jesus did. It's like having the best cheat code for life, except it's not cheating at all!

The Deep Stats vs. Real Skills Debate

Okay, here's something funny - imagine spending hours learning everything about basketball, memorizing all the stats, knowing every player's shoe size... but never actually playing the game! 🏀 That would be pretty weird, right?

Well, some people do the same thing with faith. They get super wrapped up in complicated discussions about deep religious stuff (like how many angels can dance on a pizza 😃), but they forget about the simple, important things - like being kind to others and helping people who need it.

Here's a truth bomb: You don't need to be a theological Einstein to be a good follower of Jesus. What matters more is having a good heart and taking action!

The Ultimate Life Hack

Want to know the biggest secret to happiness? It's not:

- Getting a million V-bucks
- Having the latest PlayStation
- Being TikTok famous
- Having the coolest sneakers

The real secret is loving God and serving Him only. Everything else is just temporary bonus content!

LOL Moment: The Vanity Fair
Imagine spending all your money on a super rare skin in Fortnite, and then the next day, nobody plays Fortnite anymore! That's kind of what it's like when we chase after things that don't really matter.

Here are some things that are totally "sus":
- Wanting to be rich just to show off
- Trying to become famous for no good reason
- Following trends just because everyone else is
- Thinking you're better than others

Action Items (Your Quest Log):
1. Daily Challenge: Do one kind thing for someone else without telling anyone about it
2. Squad Goals: Find a friend who helps you be a better person
3. Boss Fight: Identify one "vanity" thing in your life and try to care about it less
4. Achievement Hunt: Try to go one whole day thinking about others more than yourself

Reflection Questions (Level Up Your Thinking):
- If Jesus had a YouTube channel, would you subscribe? Why?
- What's one thing you spend too much time worrying about that probably doesn't matter?
- How can you use your favorite hobby to help others?
- If you had to choose between being the richest kid in school or the kindest, which would you pick and why?

The Epic Fail Moment
You know how in games you sometimes fail a mission and have to restart? Life is kind of like that too! We all mess up sometimes, but Jesus gives us infinite respawns to try again and do better. The key is learning from our mistakes and keeping our eyes on the prize!

Pro Gamer Tips:
1. Prayer is like a daily power-up - don't skip it!
2. Reading the Bible is like reading the game manual - it helps you understand how to play better

3. Going to church is like joining a multiplayer server with your squad
4. Helping others is like sharing your extra loot - it makes the whole game better for everyone

Final Boss Thought

Remember: Being popular on Earth is like having a high score on an old game nobody plays anymore. But being good in God's eyes? That's the real victory royale! 🏆

Weekly Challenge:

This week, try to be more like Jesus in your own unique way. Maybe you're good at making people laugh - use that to cheer up someone who's sad. Good at sports? Help someone who's struggling to learn. Great at video games? Use that patience to help a younger sibling with homework.

Remember, following Jesus isn't about being boring or perfect - it's about being the best version of yourself and helping others along the way. It's like being part of the most amazing squad ever, where everyone has each other's back!

Stay epic, and don't forget to thank your Squad Leader for all the blessings! 🙏

#SquadJesus #EpicFaith #LevelUpYourLife #BlessedGamer

How'd that mission briefing feel? Ready to take on the challenge? Drop a comment below with your thoughts! (Just kidding, this isn't YouTube, but seriously, think about it! 😊)

Chapter 2: The Ultimate Guide to Not Being a Show-Off!

Yo squad! Ready for some real talk about something we ALL struggle with? Today we're diving into why being humble is actually the most boss move you can make!

The Knowledge Trap: When Being Smart Makes You Stupid 🫠

Picture this hilarious scene: There's this kid who memorized the entire periodic table, knows every Pokémon's stats by heart, and can recite pi to 100 digits. Impressive, right? But then he goes around making everyone feel dumb and won't shut up about how smart he is. Not so cool anymore, huh?

Here's the thing - being smart is awesome! But being a know-it-all? That's about as popular as socks with sandals! 😄

The Humble Farmer vs. The Smart Aleck

Check this out: Who would you rather hang out with?

- A chill farmer who doesn't know quantum physics but is always ready to help and listen
- A "genius" who keeps correcting everyone's grammar and rolling their eyes at "less intelligent" people

The answer's pretty obvious, right? That's because humility is like having a super-power that makes everyone actually want to be around you!

The Epic Plot Twist 🌟

Here's something that'll blow your mind: The more you actually know, the more you realize how much you DON'T know! It's like leveling up in a game only to discover there are way more levels than you thought!

The Self-Roast Section 😊

Want to level up in humility? Here's your daily checklist:

1. Can you laugh at yourself when you mess up?
2. Do you admit when you don't know something?
3. Are you okay with someone else being better than you at something?
4. Can you say "I was wrong" without dying inside?

Action Items (Your Mission, Should You Choose to Accept It):
Daily Quests:

1. Try learning something new from someone younger than you
2. When you're tempted to brag, hit the mental pause button
3. Ask someone else about their interests instead of talking about yours
4. Thank someone who helped you (even if it was just a small thing)

Boss Level Challenges:
1. Let someone else win an argument (even if you're right!)
2. Ask for help with something (even if you could figure it out yourself)
3. Share credit for something good you did

The Hilarious Truth Bombs 💣
- Being humble doesn't mean thinking you're garbage
- It means being honest about your strengths AND weaknesses
- It's like having a balanced character build in an RPG!

Real Life Side Quests:

The "Actually" Challenge:
Try going a whole day without starting a sentence with "Actually..." (Harder than it sounds!)

The Ninja Compliment Mission:
Give three genuine compliments without mentioning yourself at all

The Silent Victory Dance:
Do something awesome and don't tell anyone about it (Super hard mode: Don't even post it on social media! 😬)

Reflection Questions (No Cheat Codes Allowed):
1. Why do you think it's so tempting to show off when we're good at something?
2. Have you ever felt bad because someone else was bragging? How did it feel?
3. What's the difference between being proud of yourself and being prideful?

4. If you could be the best in the world at something but nobody knew except you, would you still want it?

The LOL Learning Moments:
Remember that time you thought you knew everything about something and then found out you were totally wrong? That's not a fail - that's a learning opportunity! (But it's still pretty funny! 😉)

Pro Gamer Tips for Staying Humble:
   1. Treat everyone like they could teach you something (because they can!)
   2. When you win, thank the people who helped you get there
   3. When you lose, thank the people who taught you something new
   4. Remember: Even Jesus washed his disciples' feet, and He was literally GOD!

The Ultimate Power Move:
Want to know the most galaxy-brain move of all? The more awesome you are at something, the more humble you should be about it. It's like having an amazing secret power but acting like it's no big deal!

Weekly Challenge: Operation Under-Cover Boss
This week, try to do as many good things as possible WITHOUT getting credit for them. It's like being a secret agent of awesomeness! Keep a private score if you want, but don't tell anyone!

Emergency Humble Button ●
If you ever feel like you're getting too full of yourself, remember this:
   • Every expert was once a complete beginner
   • There's always someone better at something
   • The wisest people are usually the most humble
   • Having a big ego is like wearing a "Kiss Me I'm Awesome" t-shirt - nobody's impressed! 😊

Final Thought:
Being humble isn't about being weak or pretending you're not good at stuff. It's about being so secure in who you are that you

don't need to prove it to anyone! Now that's what I call a pro gamer move!

Remember: The most impressive people are usually the ones who aren't trying to impress anyone!

Stay humble, stay awesome, and keep leveling up your character stats in all the right ways!

#HumbleNotWeak #SecretAgent #NinjaHumility #EpicLife

Now go forth and be mysteriously awesome! 😎

Chapter 3: Truth-Seeker Mode: ACTIVATED!

Hey there, junior truth detectives! Ready to unlock the ultimate cheat code to understanding what REALLY matters? Buckle up, because this chapter is about to blow your mind like a Minecraft TNT explosion! 💥

The Great Knowledge Race 🏃‍♂️

You know how in video games sometimes you spend hours collecting every single coin or item, but then realize none of it actually helps you win the game? Well, check this out - a lot of people do the same thing with knowledge!

The Hilarious Knowledge Collector

Picture this: There's this kid who knows...

- Every Pokémon evolution
- All Marvel Universe storylines
- Complete stats of every NBA player
- Every TikTok dance move

But then can't figure out...

- How to be a good friend
- Why kindness matters
- What makes people actually happy
- How to find real peace

Pretty sus, right? ☐

The Ultimate Plot Twist

Here's the thing that'll make your brain explode: The most important truth isn't found in your textbooks, YouTube tutorials, or even your favorite streamer's channel. It comes straight from the source - God himself!

LOL Moment: The Great Debate

Imagine two kids arguing about what's inside a wrapped present:

- Kid 1: "It's definitely a PlayStation 5!"
- Kid 2: "No way, it's an Xbox Series X!" Meanwhile, the gift-giver is standing right there saying, "Actually, it's..." But they're too busy arguing to listen! 😂

The Simple Truth Challenge

Want to know what's cooler than winning an argument? Understanding these epic truth bombs:
1. One word from God > All the TikTok wisdom in the world
2. Real truth makes you free (like getting unlimited lives in a game!)
3. Simple truth > Complicated confusion

Action Items (Your Truth-Seeking Missions):
Daily Quests:
1. Ask God one question and actually wait for an answer
2. Find one simple truth and try to live it
3. Notice when you're making things more complicated than they need to be

Boss Level Challenges:
1. Give up an argument even when you're right (Super Hard Mode!)
2. Listen twice as much as you talk
3. Look for truth in unexpected places

The Truth-O-Meter Test ✏️
How to know if something is really true:
- Does it match what God says?
- Does it make you a better person?
- Would you tell your grandma about it?
- Does it still make sense when you're alone?

Hilarious Truth Fails 😄
Things people often think are super important but really aren't:
- Having the last word
- Proving you're right
- Knowing more random facts than your friends
- Being able to quote every meme ever

Reflection Questions (No Googling Allowed!):
1. What's one "truth" you believed that turned out to be totally wrong?
2. If you could ask God one question and get a clear answer, what would it be?
3. Why do you think simple truth is sometimes harder to accept than complicated explanations?

4. What's more important: winning an argument or finding the truth?

Pro Gamer Tips for Truth Seeking:
1. Truth isn't about having the most knowledge - it's about knowing what matters
2. When in doubt, keep it simple
3. Listen to God first, Google second
4. Sometimes the best answer is "I don't know"

The Ultimate Power Move: Simplicity
Want to know what's really cool? Being able to say:
- "I was wrong"
- "I need help understanding"
- "That's too complicated for me"
- "Let's ask God about this"

Weekly Challenge: Operation Truth Detective 🔍
This week's mission:
1. Find one simple truth each day
2. Try to live it out
3. Notice what happens
4. Keep a truth journal (but only if you want to - no pressure!)

Emergency Simplicity Button ●
When things get too complicated:
1. Stop
2. Breathe
3. Ask: "What would Jesus do?"
4. Do that

The Truth Seeker's Toolkit:
Essential gear for your truth-seeking adventures:
- Open mind
- Humble heart
- Listening ears
- Ready-to-learn attitude
- Sense of humor (very important!)

Final Boss Thought:
Remember: Truth isn't about knowing everything - it's about knowing what matters and living it out. It's like having the

ultimate cheat code to life, but it only works if you actually use it!

Victory Dance Move ☐

When you find a real truth:
1. Celebrate it
2. Live it
3. Share it (but don't brag about it)
4. Thank God for it

Stay true, stay awesome, and keep seeking what really matters!
#TruthSeeker #EpicLife #SimpleWisdom #GodsPlan

Remember: The best truth-seekers aren't the ones who know everything - they're the ones who know what's worth knowing! Now go forth and seek some truth! (But maybe finish your homework first! ☺)

Chapter 4: The Ultimate Guide to Not Being a Total Noob at Life Decisions!

Yo, decision-makers! Ever feel like you're playing a mega-hard game without a strategy guide? Well, grab your thinking caps because we're about to level up your life-choice skills!

The Epic Decision-Making Adventure 🧱
The Hilarious "Just Wing It" Fail

Picture this: You're playing Minecraft, and you decide to fight the Ender Dragon with:

- No armor
- A wooden sword
- Three cookies for health
- "Good vibes"

How's that gonna work out? 😊 Yeah... that's exactly how some people make life decisions!

The Not-So-Smart Smart Moves

Here's some things people do that seem smart but are actually pretty sus:

1. Believing everything they read online
2. Following the crowd without thinking
3. Making choices based on what looks cool on social media
4. Deciding stuff without praying about it first

Pro Gamer Moves for Smart Choices
The WWJD Strategy Guide:

1. Stop and think (Revolutionary, right? 😄)
2. Ask yourself: "Would Jesus facepalm at this decision?"
3. Pray about it (Like having a direct line to the ultimate strategy guide!)
4. Get advice from people who actually know what they're talking about

Action Items (Your Decision-Making Side Quests):
Daily Challenges:

1. Make one decision today that doesn't involve following the crowd

2. Wait 10 minutes before responding to something that makes you mad
3. Ask an adult you trust for advice about something (They're like walking cheat codes!)

Boss Level Missions:
1. Write down three decisions you need to make
2. Pray about them BEFORE deciding
3. Get wisdom from someone who's been there

The LOL Learning Moments 😀
Common Decision Fails:
- Choosing what to wear based on TikTok trends (RIP bank account)
- Picking friends based on their Instagram followers
- Doing something dumb just because "everyone else is doing it"
- Making choices without thinking about the consequences (Hello, bad haircut decisions!)

Reflection Questions (Think Tank Time):
1. What's the worst decision you've made because you didn't think it through?
2. Have you ever made a good choice that everyone else thought was weird?
3. What's your usual process for making decisions? (Be honest - even if it's "eeny, meeny, miny, moe"!)
4. How often do you ask God for help with choices?

The Decision-Making Toolbox □
Essential Equipment:
- Brain (Please use, not optional!)
- Prayer hotline to God (Always free, never busy)
- Wise friends and family (Your personal advisory board)
- Patience (Yes, you actually have to wait sometimes)

Weekly Challenge: Operation Smart Choice
This week, before making ANY decision bigger than what socks to wear:
1. Stop
2. Think
3. Pray

4. Ask for advice
5. THEN decide

Emergency Decision Protocol 🪦

When you're about to make a snap decision:
1. Hit the pause button
2. Take three deep breaths
3. Ask yourself: "Would this make a funny story... in a bad way?"
4. Consider: "Would Jesus share this on His Instagram?"

The Wisdom Power-Ups

Ways to level up your decision-making skills:
1. Read the Bible (It's like the ultimate strategy guide)
2. Learn from others' fails (Way less painful than learning from your own!)
3. Practice patience (Hardest skill to master, but totally worth it)
4. Keep a decision journal (Document your epic wins AND fails)

Boss Battle Tips:

When facing a tough decision:
1. Don't panic (Seriously, don't)
2. Remember you're not alone
3. Take your time (Unless it's actually life or death)
4. Ask for help (It's not cheating, it's being smart!)

The Victory Dance Checklist ✅

You know you've made a good decision when:
- You have peace about it
- Wise people agree it's smart
- It doesn't involve hiding anything from your parents
- You wouldn't be embarrassed if Jesus saw you do it

Final Boss Thought:

Making good decisions isn't about being perfect - it's about being wise enough to think things through and humble enough to ask for help!

Bonus Round: Quick Decision Test

Before making a choice, ask:
1. Is it wise?

2. Is it kind?
3. Would I want everyone to know about it?
4. Would Jesus approve? If you answer "no" to any of these, maybe hit that pause button!

Stay wise, stay awesome, and don't forget to think before you leap!

#WiseChoices #EpicDecisions #ThinkFirst #WWJDmoment

Remember: The best decisions aren't always the most popular ones, but they're the ones you won't regret posting about later! Now go forth and make some epic choices! (But maybe ask your parents first! ☺)

Chapter 5: How to Level Up Your Bible Reading Game!

What's up, divine adventurers! Ready to transform boring Bible reading into an epic quest for truth? Let's turn this into the most awesome reading adventure ever! 🎮

The Ultimate Reading Strategy Guide 🎮

Common Bible Reading Fails:
- Opening the Bible randomly and pointing at a verse (It's not a fortune cookie, bro! 😊)
- Reading only when you're in trouble (The Bible isn't just a spiritual emergency hotline!)
- Falling asleep every time you try to read (We've all been there!)
- Reading without actually thinking about what it means

The Epic Truth Bomb 💣

Here's something mind-blowing: The Bible isn't just another boring book - it's like having God's personal DMs to you! How cool is that?

What Makes Bible Reading Awesome:
1. It's packed with epic stories
2. It's full of life cheat codes
3. It helps you level up your character stats
4. It's basically God's strategy guide for life

Action Items (Your Bible Reading Quests):

Daily Missions:
1. Read one chapter (Start with Mark - it's action-packed!)
2. Find one verse that actually means something to you
3. Try to apply what you read to your day
4. Share something cool you learned with a friend

Boss Level Challenges:
1. Start a Bible reading streak
2. Create a Bible verse meme (Keep it respectful!)
3. Read with a friend and discuss
4. Start a Bible journal with awesome discoveries

The LOL Learning Moments 😄

Things Not to Do:

- Don't use the Bible to win arguments
- Don't just read the "popular" verses
- Don't treat it like a magic 8-ball
- Don't skip the "boring" parts (They're actually important!)

Pro Gamer Tips for Bible Reading:
The S.W.O.R.D. Method:
- **S**top and pray before reading
- **W**atch for cool details
- **O**bserve what it means
- **R**eflect on how it applies to you
- **D**o what it says

Weekly Challenge: Operation Bible Explorer 🔍
This week's mission:
1. Pick a book of the Bible (Maybe start with John!)
2. Read one chapter each day
3. Write down one thing that stands out
4. Try to live it out
5. Share your discoveries with someone

Reflection Questions (No Wrong Answers!):
1. What's your favorite Bible story and why?
2. If you could hang out with any Bible character for a day, who would it be?
3. What's the coolest thing you've learned from the Bible so far?
4. How can you make Bible reading more fun?

The Bible Reader's Toolkit:
Essential gear for your Bible adventures:
- A Bible you can understand (Ask for help choosing one!)
- A journal for cool discoveries
- A curious mind
- A willing heart
- Some awesome friends to discuss with

Emergency Bible Reading Rescue 🆘
When you're stuck:
1. Pray for help understanding
2. Ask someone wise

3. Use a study Bible
4. Look up confusing words
5. Don't give up!

Fun Bible Reading Challenges:
The 7-Day Challenge:
- Day 1: Read about creation
- Day 2: Read about David and Goliath
- Day 3: Read about Daniel in the lions' den
- Day 4: Read about Jesus' birth
- Day 5: Read about Jesus' coolest miracle
- Day 6: Read about Easter
- Day 7: Pick your own adventure!

The Victory Dance Moments 🕺
Celebrate when:
- You understand something new
- You find a verse that helps you
- You complete a whole book
- You help someone else understand

Final Boss Thought:
Reading the Bible isn't about being perfect - it's about getting to know God better and becoming more awesome at life!

Bonus Round: Make It Fun!
Ways to enjoy Bible reading:
1. Read it like a movie script
2. Draw the stories
3. Make it into a comic
4. Act it out with friends
5. Create a soundtrack for different stories

Stay curious, stay awesome, and keep leveling up your Bible knowledge!

#BibleAdventure #EpicTruth #GodSquad #LevelUpLife

Remember: The Bible isn't just an ancient book - it's your guide to becoming the epic person God created you to be! Now go forth and start reading! (And yes, the book of Revelation is totally wild! 🤪)

P.S. - Don't forget to ask your parents or youth leader if you need help understanding something. They're like your spiritual tech support! 😎
CopyRetry

Chapter 6: How to Stop Being a Slave to Your Likes and Wants!

Yo epic gamers of life! Ever feel like you're totally controlled by what you want? Like your desires are the boss battle you can't beat? Let's learn how to be the player, not the NPC in your own life!

The Desire Dilemma ♂️
The Hilarious Want-Monster Syndrome:
Picture this: You're like a character who:
- MUST have every new skin in Fortnite
- CAN'T RESIST checking your phone every 2 minutes
- NEEDS the latest everything
- Gets grumpy when you don't get what you want

Sound familiar? (Don't worry, we've all been there! 😄)

The Epic Battle: You vs. Your Wants
Imagine your desires are like a clingy pet that follows you everywhere:
- "Buy this!"
- "Play more games!"
- "One more YouTube video!"
- "I NEED those new sneakers!"

The Not-So-Secret Secret
Here's the mind-blowing truth: Real freedom isn't getting everything you want - it's being okay when you don't! ☐

Power Moves for Controlling Your Wants:
1. Learn to say "nah" to yourself
2. Find joy in simple things
3. Be grateful for what you have
4. Think before you want

Action Items (Your Self-Control Side Quests):
Daily Challenges:
1. Say "no" to one thing you want but don't need
2. Wait 24 hours before buying something "cool"
3. Share something instead of keeping it all
4. Be happy for someone else's success

Boss Level Missions:
1. Give away something you like
2. Fast from your favorite game/app for a day
3. Save money instead of spending it
4. Help someone else without wanting anything back

The LOL Learning Moments 😂
Common Desire Fails:
- Spending all your money on V-bucks
- Getting mad when your WiFi is slow
- Being jealous of your friend's new stuff
- Throwing a fit when you don't get your way

Reflection Questions (Truth Time!):
1. What's one thing you want RIGHT NOW that you probably don't need?
2. Have you ever gotten something you really wanted and then got bored with it?
3. What's something you have that you're truly thankful for?
4. How do you feel when you can't have what you want?

The Self-Control Toolbox 🧰
Essential Equipment:
- Patience (Level 1 - but can be upgraded!)
- Gratitude glasses (To see what you already have)
- The power button (Yes, you can actually turn things off!)
- The word "NO" (Your new superpower!)

Weekly Challenge: Operation Want-Less
This week, try:
1. Making a gratitude list
2. Waiting before getting something new
3. Finding fun in free things

4. Being content with what you have

Emergency Desire Control Protocol 👻

When you're about to lose it because you want something:
1. Take a deep breath
2. Count to 10
3. Ask: "Do I really need this?"
4. Remember what you're grateful for

Victory Conditions ✨

You know you're winning when:
- You can say "no" to yourself
- You're happy with what you have
- You can wait for things
- You enjoy making others happy

Boss Battle Tips:

When fighting the Want-Monster:
1. Remember you're stronger than your desires
2. Think about others
3. Pray for help
4. Find joy in giving

The Ultimate Power Move

Want to be really cool? Learn to be happy with less! It's like having an unbeatable superpower that no one can take away!

Bonus Round: Happiness Hack

Things that actually make you happy:
- Friends who like you for YOU
- Helping others
- Being grateful
- Growing stronger in character

Final Boss Thought:

Being in control of your wants doesn't mean you can't have nice things - it means nice things don't control you!

Victory Dance Checklist ✅

You're winning when:
- You can wait patiently
- You enjoy what you have
- You can share easily
- You're not controlled by your wants

Stay strong, stay awesome, and keep leveling up your self-control!

#SelfControl #EpicLife #WantLess #LiveMore

Remember: The most powerful person isn't the one who has everything they want - it's the one who's happy without needing everything! Now go forth and conquer those wants! (But maybe keep the pizza cravings... those are legit! ☺🍕)

P.S. - If you're struggling with wanting too much stuff, talk to your parents or a trusted adult. They've probably fought this boss battle before and have some epic strategies to share!

Chapter 7: How to Drop the Ego and Level Up Your Humility!

Wassup future saints! Ready to learn how NOT to be that person everyone rolls their eyes at? Let's dive into the ultimate guide to crushing pride and becoming genuinely awesome!

The Pride Problem ⚲

The Classic Pride Fails:

Imagine being that kid who:
- Has to win EVERY argument
- Brags about EVERYTHING
- Makes every story about themselves
- Can't handle being wrong... ever
- Posts #Blessed but really means #BetterThanYou

Sound like anyone you know? (Maybe even... yourself sometimes? 😄)

The Epic Plot Twist ✸

Here's the mind-blowing truth: True confidence doesn't need to show off! It's like having an awesome rare item in a game but not needing to equip it just to flex!

Signs You Might Be Playing on Pride Mode:
1. You hate being wrong
2. You make up excuses for everything

3. You feel threatened when others succeed
4. You have to be the best at everything
5. You can't laugh at yourself

Action Items (Your Humility Quest):
Daily Missions:
1. Let someone else win an argument
2. Admit when you're wrong
3. Congratulate someone who beats you
4. Ask for help (even if you think you don't need it)

Boss Level Challenges:
1. Keep your achievements secret for a week
2. Let someone else take credit for something
3. Learn from someone younger than you
4. Do something nice without posting about it

The LOL Learning Moments 😊
Pride Fails That Make Everyone Cringe:
- Starting every sentence with "Actually..."
- Making up fake stories to sound cool
- Posting humble-brag selfies
- Never admitting mistakes

Reflection Questions (Get Real Time!):
1. When was the last time you felt the need to show off? Why?
2. What's harder: being wrong or admitting you're wrong?
3. Do you feel bad when others succeed?
4. How often do you make things about yourself?

The Humility Toolbox 🧰
Essential Equipment:
- The ability to say "I was wrong"
- A sense of humor about yourself
- Joy in others' success
- The power to stay quiet about your wins

Weekly Challenge: Operation Humble Heart
This week's mission:
1. Do three good things secretly
2. Let others shine
3. Listen more than you talk

4. Find ways to help without taking credit

Emergency Pride Control Protocol
When pride is about to make you act sus:
1. Remember everyone makes mistakes
2. Think about how you'd feel in their shoes
3. Ask yourself: "Would Jesus facepalm at this?"
4. Take a humility check

Victory Dance Moments
You're winning at humility when:
- You can laugh at your own fails
- You're happy when others succeed
- You don't need to prove yourself
- You can admit when you're wrong

Boss Battle Tips:
Fighting pride like a pro:
1. Remember you're not the main character in everyone else's story
2. It's okay not to be the best
3. Your worth isn't in your achievements
4. God loves you no matter what

The Ultimate Power Move
Want to be actually cool? Be the person who:
- Builds others up
- Admits mistakes
- Shares the spotlight
- Stays humble when winning

Bonus Round: The Humble Flex
Things that are actually impressive:
- Being kind when no one's watching
- Helping others succeed
- Learning from everyone
- Being real about your fails

Final Boss Thought:
True greatness isn't about being better than others - it's about being better than you were yesterday and helping others along the way!

The Secret Strategy Guide

Ways to level up your humility:
1. Thank God for your talents
2. Remember where your gifts came from
3. Use your skills to help others
4. Stay teachable always

Stay humble, stay real, and keep growing in grace!
#HumbleHeart #RealTalk #GrowthMindset #BlessedForReal
Remember: The most impressive people are usually the ones who aren't trying to impress anyone! Now go forth and be awesome... quietly! ☺

P.S. - If pride is a boss battle you keep losing, talk to God about it. He's pretty good at helping with this stuff (and He definitely won't post about it on social media! 😊)

Chapter 8: The Ultimate Guide to Not Being BFFs with EVERYONE!

Hey squad! Ready for some real talk about friendship? Today's mission: learning how to pick your friends wisely without being a total snob! Let's dive into the epic guide of friendship wisdom!

The Friendship Trap ⚔️
Common Friend Fails:
Picture this kid who:
- Tells EVERYONE their secrets
- Tries to be besties with the whole school
- Can't keep any private info private
- Changes personality for each friend group
- Says "We're basically family!" after one hangout

Sound familiar? (We've all been there! 😊)

The Epic Truth Bomb 💣
Here's the mind-blowing reality: Not everyone needs to be your BFF! It's like having a friends list in a game - you don't need to accept EVERY request!

Friendship Levels (Like a Game):
1. Level 1: Acquaintances (NPCs)

2. Level 2: School Friends
3. Level 3: Good Friends
4. Level 4: Close Friends
5. LEGENDARY Level: True Best Friends

Action Items (Your Friendship Quest):
Daily Missions:
1. Keep one secret (even small ones!)
2. Be real with your true friends
3. Think before sharing personal stuff
4. Stay loyal to your real squad

Boss Level Challenges:
1. Evaluate your friendship circle
2. Set healthy boundaries
3. Be a good friend without oversharing
4. Learn to say "no" to toxic friendships

The LOL Learning Moments 😂
Classic Friendship Fails:
- Spilling all the tea to everyone
- Being "best friends" with someone you met yesterday
- Sharing private convos in the group chat
- Having zero boundaries

Reflection Questions (Friend Check Time!):
1. Who are your real ride-or-die friends?
2. Do you change who you are for different friends?
3. Can you keep secrets?
4. Do your friends make you a better person?

The Friendship Toolbox 🧰
Essential Equipment:
- Good judgment
- Loyalty
- The ability to keep secrets
- Healthy boundaries
- Real friendship skills

Weekly Challenge: Operation True Friend
This week, try:
1. Being extra loyal to real friends
2. Keeping private things private

3. Being the same person with everyone
4. Standing up for your true friends

Emergency Friendship Protocol
When you're tempted to overshare or people-please:
1. Stop and think
2. Ask: "Would a real friend do this?"
3. Remember your loyalty
4. Consider long-term consequences

Victory Dance Moments
You're winning at friendship when:
- You have a solid core friend group
- You can keep secrets
- You're known as trustworthy
- You're real with your friends

Boss Battle Tips:
For fighting friendship drama:
1. Quality > Quantity
2. True friends > Popular friends
3. Real connections > Social media followers
4. Being yourself > Being liked by everyone

The Ultimate Power Move
Want to be a legendary friend? Be someone who:
- Keeps their word
- Stays loyal
- Tells the truth (kindly)
- Makes others better

Bonus Round: Friend Filter
Good friends:
- Build you up
- Keep your secrets
- Tell you the truth
- Point you to God

Final Boss Thought:
It's better to have a few real friends than a hundred fake ones! Quality friendship is about depth, not numbers!

The Secret Strategy Guide
How to build real friendships:

1. Be genuine
2. Stay loyal
3. Keep confidences
4. Choose wisely
5. Put God first

Stay true, stay loyal, and keep building those real friendships! #RealFriends #TrueSquad #LoyaltyOverLikes #GenuineFriendship

Remember: The best friends aren't the ones who know all your secrets - they're the ones who keep them! Now go be an epic friend! ☺

P.S. - If you're struggling with friendship stuff, talk to a parent or trusted adult. They've probably dealt with similar challenges and might have some epic wisdom to share! Plus, Jesus is the ultimate friend who never lets you down! 🙏

Chapter 9: The Epic Guide to Being a Good Team Player!

Yo future saints! Ready to learn how to level up your obedience game without being a total pushover? Let's dive into the ultimate guide to following the rules while staying cool!

The Obedience Challenge ♂

Common Rebellion Fails:

Picture being that kid who:
- Always has to do things their way
- Thinks rules are "just suggestions"
- Can't take direction
- Gets mad when told what to do
- Has to be the boss of everything

(If you're cringing because this sounds familiar, don't worry - we've got the cheat codes! 😊)

The Mind-Blowing Truth 🌟

Here's the plot twist: Real strength isn't about doing whatever you want - it's about having the courage to follow good leadership! It's like being part of an epic raid team in an MMO!

Why Obedience is Actually Cool:
1. It shows you're secure enough to follow
2. It helps you learn from others' experience
3. It makes you part of something bigger
4. It levels up your character stats!

Action Items (Your Obedience Quest):
Daily Missions:
1. Follow one rule you usually ignore
2. Listen to instructions without arguing
3. Do what you're told the first time
4. Thank someone who leads you

Boss Level Challenges:
1. Accept correction without getting defensive
2. Follow directions even when you think you know better
3. Support your team leader's decisions
4. Help others follow the rules too

The LOL Learning Moments 😊
Classic Rebellion Fails:
- Getting in trouble for "knowing better"
- Missing out because you wouldn't listen
- Making things harder by being stubborn
- Learning lessons the hard way

Reflection Questions (Real Talk Time!):
1. Why do you hate being told what to do?
2. Have you ever regretted not following instructions?
3. Who are the good leaders in your life?
4. How could being more obedient make your life easier?

The Obedience Toolbox 🧰
Essential Equipment:
- Humble heart
- Listening ears
- Patient spirit
- Willing attitude
- Team player mindset

Weekly Challenge: Operation Good Follower
This week's mission:
1. Follow instructions immediately
2. Don't argue with directions
3. Support your leaders
4. Help create team unity

Emergency Rebellion Control 🚨
When you feel like rebelling:
1. Take a deep breath
2. Remember you're part of a team
3. Think about the consequences
4. Choose wisdom over pride

Victory Dance Moments ☐
You're winning at obedience when:
- You follow directions first time
- You help create peace
- You make leaders' jobs easier
- You're known as reliable

Boss Battle Tips:
Fighting the rebellion boss:
1. Remember everyone answers to someone
2. Even Jesus followed rules
3. Good followers make good leaders
4. Team success > Personal pride

The Ultimate Power Move
Want to be genuinely respected? Be someone who:
- Follows well
- Supports others
- Creates unity
- Makes things better

Bonus Round: Leadership Levels
Good followers:
- Make teams stronger
- Help others succeed
- Create positive vibes
- Build up the squad

Final Boss Thought:

Following well isn't about being weak - it's about being strong enough to be part of something bigger than yourself!
The Secret Strategy Guide 📖
Ways to level up your following skills:
    1. Listen first
    2. Act quickly
    3. Support others
    4. Stay humble
    5. Keep learning

Stay cool, stay humble, and keep being an awesome team player!
#TeamPlayer #SquadGoals #UnityOverPride #WinningTogether
Remember: The best team members aren't always the stars - they're the ones who make the whole team better! Now go forth and be an epic follower! ☺

P.S. - If you're struggling with authority, remember that even Jesus followed His Father's plan. That makes following good leadership pretty cool! 🙇

Chapter 10: How to Not Be That Kid Who Never Shuts Up!

What's up, future saints! Time to tackle the epic boss battle of learning when to zip it! Let's master the legendary art of NOT talking everyone's ears off!

The Chatterbox Challenge 🗯️
Common Talk Fails:
Picture that kid who:
 • Interrupts EVERYONE
 • Shares every thought that pops into their head
 • Can't handle silence
 • Spills all the tea without thinking
 • Makes every conversation about themselves

(If you're feeling called out right now... same! 😅)
The Epic Truth Bomb 💣

39

Here's the mind-blowing reality: Sometimes the most powerful move is NOT saying anything! It's like having an ultimate power move but saving it for the right moment!

Why Silence is Actually Your Superpower:
1. It makes your words mean more
2. It helps you learn cool stuff
3. It keeps you out of drama
4. It makes you seem mysterious and wise 😎

Action Items (Your Quiet Quest):
Daily Missions:
1. Count to 5 before speaking
2. Keep one thought to yourself
3. Listen twice as much as you talk
4. Have a quiet time challenge

Boss Level Challenges:
1. Go one hour without talking (except when needed)
2. Listen to someone's whole story without interrupting
3. Keep a cool secret
4. Think before sharing

The LOL Learning Moments 😆
Classic Talking Fails:
- Spilling someone else's secret
- Saying something embarrassing because you didn't think
- Getting in trouble for talking too much in class
- Ruining surprises because you couldn't keep quiet

Reflection Questions (Silent Think Time!):
1. Do you talk more than you listen?
2. Have you ever wished you could take back words?
3. What's the longest you can stay quiet?
4. Do you feel uncomfortable with silence?

The Quiet Toolbox 🧰
Essential Equipment:
- Self-control button
- Patience meter
- Listening skills
- Think-before-you-speak filter

Weekly Challenge: Operation Golden Silence
This week, try:
1. Having a daily quiet time
2. Listening more than talking
3. Keeping some thoughts private
4. Using fewer words

Emergency Chatterbox Control
When you can't stop talking:
1. Take a deep breath
2. Count to 10
3. Ask yourself: "Does this need to be said?"
4. Remember: Silence is golden!

Victory Dance Moments
You know you're winning when:
- You can keep secrets
- People trust you with information
- You're known as a good listener
- You think before you speak

Boss Battle Tips:
Fighting the urge to talk:
1. Pretend your words cost money
2. Imagine everything's being recorded
3. Think about consequences
4. Remember less is more

The Ultimate Power Move
Want to be really impressive? Be the one who:
- Listens well
- Speaks wisely
- Keeps confidence
- Creates peaceful vibes

Bonus Round: Speech Stats
Your words should be:
- True
- Helpful
- Important
- Kind

Final Boss Thought:

Being quiet isn't about being boring - it's about making your words count when you do speak!

The Secret Strategy Guide 📖

How to level up your quiet game:
1. Practice listening
2. Value silence
3. Think first
4. Speak last

Stay cool, stay thoughtful, and keep those unnecessary words in check!

#QuietStrength #WiseWords #ListenMore #TalkLess

Remember: The most interesting people aren't always the loudest - sometimes they're the ones who know when to be quiet! Now go forth and practice your ninja silence skills! ☺

P.S. - If you're struggling with talking too much, try setting small quiet-time goals. Start with 5 minutes and work your way up. And remember, Jesus often went to quiet places to pray - that makes silence pretty epic! 🙏

Chapter 11: How to Level Up Your Inner Peace Game!

Yo peace seekers! Ready to learn how to stay chill when life gets crazy? Let's master the art of keeping your cool like a true spiritual ninja!

The Peace Challenge 🧨
Common Peace Fails:
Picture that kid who:
- Freaks out over every little thing
- Can't handle when WiFi is slow
- Gets mad when plans change
- Stress-eats during tests
- Rage quits when losing games

(If you're feeling personally attacked... don't worry, we've got solutions! 😊)

The Epic Truth Bomb 💣
Here's the secret: Real peace isn't about having a perfect life - it's about staying cool when life gets sus! It's like having an invisible shield against chaos!

Why Inner Peace is Your Ultimate Powerup:
1. Makes you unstoppable in tough times
2. Helps you think clearly
3. Keeps you from making dumb decisions
4. Makes you look like a total boss

Action Items (Your Peace Quest):
Daily Missions:
1. Take 3 deep breaths when stressed
2. Find one quiet moment
3. Say a quick prayer when worried
4. Choose not to freak out

Boss Level Challenges:
1. Stay calm when someone's annoying
2. Handle a disappointment without drama
3. Keep cool during a test
4. Be patient in a long line

The LOL Learning Moments 😄

Classic Peace Fails:
- Having a meltdown over lost gaming time
- Screaming at siblings over nothing
- Throwing the controller when losing
- Stress-eating an entire pizza

Reflection Questions (Chill Think Time!):
1. What makes you lose your peace?
2. How do you usually react to problems?
3. What helps you calm down?
4. Who's the most peaceful person you know?

The Peace Toolbox 🧰

Essential Equipment:
- Deep breathing skills
- Prayer hotline
- Patience power-ups
- Chill pill inventory

Weekly Challenge: Operation Inner Calm

This week's mission:
1. Create a peaceful morning routine
2. Find a quiet spot for thinking
3. Practice staying calm in annoying situations
4. Help others find peace

Emergency Peace Protocol 🆘

When you're about to lose it:
1. Stop
2. Breathe
3. Pray
4. Remember it's not the end of the world

Victory Dance Moments 💃

You're winning at peace when:
- Small problems don't wreck your day
- You help others stay calm
- You can handle changes
- You're known as the chill one

Boss Battle Tips:

Fighting stress like a pro:
1. Remember God's got your back

2. Take one thing at a time
3. Focus on what you can control
4. Let go of what you can't

The Ultimate Power Move
Want to be legendarily peaceful? Be someone who:
- Stays calm in chaos
- Helps others find peace
- Doesn't stress the small stuff
- Trusts God's plan

Bonus Round: Peace Stats
True peace comes from:
- Knowing God's in control
- Accepting what you can't change
- Taking care of your spirit
- Helping others find calm

Final Boss Thought:
Peace isn't about having an easy life - it's about having an unshakeable spirit!

The Secret Strategy Guide 📖
Ways to level up your peace:
1. Start your day with God
2. Take regular quiet breaks
3. Choose your battles
4. Trust the process
5. Help others find peace

Stay cool, stay peaceful, and keep that inner calm strong!
#InnerPeace #ChillVibes #SpiritualNinja #GodsPeace
Remember: The most powerful people aren't those who never face storms - they're the ones who stay peaceful during them! Now go forth and spread those chill vibes! ☺
P.S. - If you're struggling to find peace, remember Jesus could sleep through a storm on a boat. That's the kind of peace we're aiming for! Talk to Him about it - He's pretty good at sharing His peace! 🙏

Chapter 12: How to Level Up Through Life's Hard Stuff!

Yo future warriors! Ready to learn how to turn life's difficulties into power-ups? Let's discover how tough times can actually make you more epic!

The Adversity Challenge 🎮

Common Difficulty Fails:

Picture that kid who:
- Gives up at the first obstacle
- Complains about everything hard
- Blames others for problems
- Expects life to be easy mode
- Rage quits when facing challenges

(If this sounds familiar, don't worry - we're about to upgrade your resilience stats! 😊)

The Epic Truth Bomb 💣

Here's the mind-blowing reality: Difficulties aren't game-overs - they're actually experience points in disguise! Every challenge is a chance to level up!

Why Hard Times Are Actually Power-Ups:
1. They make you stronger
2. They teach you cool skills
3. They show what you're made of
4. They prep you for bigger battles

Action Items (Your Tough Times Quest):

Daily Missions:
1. Face one small challenge bravely
2. Find something good in something hard
3. Thank God for a difficult lesson
4. Help someone else through their battle

Boss Level Challenges:
1. Take on a hard task without complaining
2. Learn from a failure
3. Stay positive during problems
4. Turn a setback into a comeback

The LOL Learning Moments 😄

Classic Difficulty Fails:
- Quitting because "it's too hard"
- Having a meltdown over homework
- Avoiding challenges altogether
- Making excuses instead of efforts

Reflection Questions (Growth Think Time!):
1. What's your toughest challenge right now?
2. How have past difficulties made you stronger?
3. What's the best lesson you've learned from something hard?
4. Who helps you through tough times?

The Adversity Toolbox ☐
Essential Equipment:
- Courage shield
- Persistence potion
- Prayer power-up
- Growth mindset gear

Weekly Challenge: Operation Tough Cookie
This week's mission:
1. Face fears with faith
2. Turn complaints into solutions
3. Help others be brave
4. Thank God for growth opportunities

Emergency Difficulty Protocol 🚨
When facing tough times:
1. Remember it's temporary
2. Look for the lesson
3. Pray for strength
4. Keep moving forward

Victory Dance Moments ☐
You're winning at handling difficulties when:
- Challenges excite rather than scare you
- You help others be brave
- You learn from hard times
- You stay positive in problems

Boss Battle Tips:
Fighting life's tough battles:

1. God's got your back
2. Every difficulty makes you stronger
3. You're tougher than you think
4. Growth comes through challenges

The Ultimate Power Move
Want to be legendarily resilient? Be someone who:
- Faces challenges with courage
- Helps others be strong
- Learns from every difficulty
- Never gives up

Bonus Round: Resilience Stats
True strength comes from:
- Trusting God's plan
- Learning from struggles
- Staying positive
- Helping others

Final Boss Thought:
Hard times don't define you - they refine you! Like a blacksmith's forge making a sword stronger!

The Secret Strategy Guide 📖
Ways to level up through difficulties:
1. Keep your faith strong
2. Find good in hard times
3. Learn from every challenge
4. Help others through their battles
5. Stay positive no matter what

Stay strong, stay brave, and keep leveling up through life's challenges!

#StrengthThroughStruggles #NeverGiveUp #LevelUpLife #GodsPlan

Remember: The most epic heroes aren't those who never face difficulties - they're the ones who grow stronger through them! Now go forth and conquer those challenges! ☺

P.S. - When life gets super tough, remember David faced Goliath with just a sling and some stones (and faith in God). Sometimes your biggest challenges lead to your biggest victories! Talk to God about your battles - He's the ultimate Guide! 🙏

Practical Challenge Box 🧩

Try these this week:
1. Start a "Victory Journal" of challenges you've overcome
2. Create a "Tough Times Playlist" of encouraging songs
3. Make a "Power-Up Prayer List" for hard moments
4. Find a "Battle Buddy" to support each other

You've got this, young warrior! Every challenge is just making you more awesome! 💪

Chapter 13: Temptation Takedown: Your Guide to Not Getting Played!

Yo future champions! Ready to learn how to dodge life's sneaky traps like a pro gamer? Let's master the art of beating temptation and staying in the game!

The Temptation Challenge ♂️

Common Temptation Fails:

Picture that kid who:
- Can't resist the last cookie (after promising not to)
- Peeks at their friend's test answers
- Says "just five more minutes" for 2 hours of gaming
- Lies to get out of trouble
- Follows the crowd doing wrong stuff

(Getting flashbacks? Don't worry - we're about to unlock some epic resistance skills! 😊)

The Epic Truth Bomb 💣

Here's the reality check: Temptations are like tutorial levels - they seem easy but can totally wreck your game if you fall for them! But guess what? You've got cheat codes (good ones, not the bad kind!)

Why Resisting Temptation Makes You Epic:
1. Shows you've got real character
2. Levels up your willpower
3. Earns respect points
4. Keeps you out of trouble

49

Action Items (Your Resistance Quest):
Daily Missions:
1. Spot your weakness triggers
2. Have an escape plan ready
3. Phone a friend when tempted
4. Pray for strength before tough situations

Boss Level Challenges:
1. Say no to a strong temptation
2. Help someone else resist
3. Create good habits to replace bad ones
4. Be honest even when lying seems easier

The LOL Learning Moments 😂
Classic Temptation Fails:
- "I'll just watch ONE more YouTube video..."
- "Nobody will know if I copy this homework..."
- "It's not really stealing if I borrow it forever..."
- "Everyone else is doing it..."

Reflection Questions (Strategy Time!):
1. What's your biggest temptation weakness?
2. Who can help you stay strong?
3. What tricks does temptation use on you?
4. What's your best resistance strategy?

The Resistance Toolbox 🧰
Essential Equipment:
- Prayer Shield
- Friend Support System
- Emergency Exit Strategy
- Willpower Power-Ups

Weekly Challenge: Operation Temptation Warrior
This week's mission:
1. Identify your trigger spots
2. Create escape routes
3. Build a support squad
4. Practice quick responses

Emergency Temptation Protocol 🚨
When temptation hits:
1. STOP

2. PRAY
3. RUN (literally if you have to!)
4. CALL FOR BACKUP

Victory Dance Moments 📖
You're winning when:
- You can say no to strong temptations
- You help others resist
- You choose right even when wrong is easier
- You're known for being trustworthy

Boss Battle Tips:
Fighting temptation like a pro:
1. Know your weak spots
2. Have backup ready
3. Remember the consequences
4. Keep your eyes on the prize

The Ultimate Power Move
Want to be legendarily strong? Be someone who:
- Resists when others give in
- Helps others stay strong
- Creates good alternatives
- Learns from mistakes

Bonus Round: Resistance Stats
True strength comes from:
- Knowing God's got your back
- Having good friends
- Planning ahead
- Learning from fails

Final Boss Thought:
You're stronger than your temptations - they only have the power you give them!

The Secret Strategy Guide 📖
Ways to level up your resistance:
1. Start each day with prayer
2. Know your triggers
3. Have multiple backup plans
4. Stay connected to good friends
5. Remember who you want to be

Stay strong, stay smart, and keep leveling up your resistance! #TemptationWarrior #StayStrong #PowerUp #GodSquad
Remember: The most epic winners aren't those who never face temptation - they're the ones who learn to beat it! Now go forth and conquer those temptations! ☺

Emergency Quick Tips Box 📱
When tempted, try:
1. The 10-Second Rule (Wait 10 seconds before deciding)
2. The Phone-A-Friend Option (Call your backup squad)
3. The Future You Test (Would future you be proud?)
4. The Jesus Check (What would He do?)

P.S. - Even Jesus faced temptations in the desert, and He used Scripture to fight back! That's a pro gamer move right there! Load up on those Bible verses - they're like special power-up codes! 🎧

Stay awesome, stay strong, and remember: Every temptation you beat makes you more powerful! 💪

Chapter 14: How to Not Be That Kid Who Judges Everyone!

Yo future saints! Time to tackle the ultimate challenge of not being the player who criticizes everyone else's game! Let's master the art of minding our own business!

The Judgment Game 🔍
Common Judgment Fails:
Picture that kid who:
- Points out EVERYONE'S mistakes
- Spreads rumors about others
- Always thinks they know better
- Makes fun of how others play
- Can't see their own faults

(If you're feeling called out, don't worry - we're about to level up your empathy stats! 😊)

The Epic Truth Bomb 💣

52

Here's the plot twist: The more you judge others, the less time you have to improve your own game! It's like trying to play someone else's character while your own is getting wrecked!

Why Not Judging Makes You Epic:
1. People actually like being around you
2. You focus on your own growth
3. You make fewer enemies
4. You become more understanding

Action Items (Your Non-Judgment Quest):

Daily Missions:
1. Find good in someone you usually criticize
2. Keep one criticism to yourself
3. Look at your own faults first
4. Help someone instead of judging them

Boss Level Challenges:
1. Go a whole day without criticizing anyone
2. Find three good things about your "rivals"
3. Admit your own mistakes
4. Defend someone being judged

The LOL Learning Moments 😊

Classic Judgment Fails:
- Getting caught doing exactly what you criticized
- Finding out you were totally wrong about someone
- Losing friends because of being too critical
- Getting a taste of your own medicine

Reflection Questions (Mirror Time!):
1. Why do you judge others?
2. How would you feel if everyone judged you?
3. What's your biggest fault that you ignore?
4. Who have you misjudged recently?

The Non-Judgment Toolbox □

Essential Equipment:
- Empathy Goggles
- Self-Reflection Mirror
- Kindness Filter
- Understanding Upgrade

Weekly Challenge: Operation Kind Mind

This week's mission:
1. Find good in everyone
2. Focus on fixing yourself
3. Stop negative comments
4. Spread positivity instead

Emergency Judgment Control 🚨

When you want to judge:
1. Check yourself first
2. Consider their story
3. Choose kindness
4. Change the subject

Victory Dance Moments ☐

You're winning when:
- You see good in others
- People trust you
- You focus on self-improvement
- You defend the judged

Boss Battle Tips:

Fighting the urge to judge:
1. Remember your own fails
2. Think "what if that was me?"
3. Look for reasons to praise
4. Mind your own game

The Ultimate Power Move

Want to be legendarily kind? Be someone who:
- Builds others up
- Sees the best in people
- Helps those who struggle
- Keeps criticisms private

Bonus Round: Kindness Stats

True wisdom shows in:
- How you treat others
- What you say about them
- How you help them grow
- When you choose silence

Final Boss Thought:

Judging others is like playing a game on hard mode while your own character needs leveling up!

The Secret Strategy Guide 📖

Ways to level up your kindness:
1. Start with self-reflection
2. Practice understanding
3. Choose encouragement
4. Keep criticisms to yourself
5. Help others improve

Stay kind, stay humble, and keep working on your own character!

#NoJudgment #KindnessWins #LevelUpLife #BeTheGood

Remember: The most impressive players aren't those who point out others' fails - they're the ones who help everyone win! Now go forth and spread that kindness! ☺

Quick Response Guide ♂

When tempted to judge, ask:
1. "Do I do this too?"
2. "What's their story?"
3. "How can I help?"
4. "What would Jesus say?"

P.S. - Remember when Jesus said "Judge not, lest ye be judged"? He was basically saying "Don't be that player who trash-talks everyone else's game!" Pretty solid advice! 🙏

Stay awesome, stay kind, and remember: Every time you choose not to judge, you're leveling up your character! 💪

Chapter 15: The Epic Guide to Being a Real-Life Hero!

Yo future good-deed champions! Ready to learn how to be an actual hero in your daily life? Let's unlock the secret power of doing good stuff for others!

The Charity Challenge 🌟

Common Hero Fails:

Picture that kid who:
- Only helps when people are watching
- Brags about every good deed
- Expects rewards for being nice
- Does good stuff just for likes
- Helps only when it's easy

(If you're feeling called out, don't sweat it - we're about to transform you into a stealth kindness ninja! 😎)

The Epic Truth Bomb 💣

Here's the mind-blowing reality: Real heroes often work in secret! It's like being an undercover agent of awesomeness! The best good deeds are often the ones nobody knows about!

Why Secret Good Deeds Are Your Superpower:
1. They show real character
2. They make a real difference
3. They give you secret joy
4. They level up your soul stats!

Action Items (Your Hero Quest):

Daily Missions:
1. Do one secret good deed
2. Help someone who can't pay you back
3. Be kind when no one's watching
4. Make someone's day better

Boss Level Challenges:
1. Help your "enemy"
2. Do chores without being asked
3. Give up something for someone else
4. Stand up for someone being picked on

The LOL Learning Moments 😄

56

Classic Good Deed Fails:
- "Did you see what I just did?!"
- Filming yourself helping homeless people
- Only being nice when crush is watching
- Helping just to post about it later

Reflection Questions (Hero Check Time!):
1. When was the last time you helped in secret?
2. Who needs your help right now?
3. What skills do you have that could help others?
4. How can you be a hero at home?

The Hero Toolbox □

Essential Equipment:
- Kindness Radar
- Helping Hands
- Secret Service Mode
- Love Power-Ups

Weekly Challenge: Operation Stealth Hero

This week's mission:
1. Do five secret good deeds
2. Help your family without being asked
3. Be extra kind to someone having a rough time
4. Share with others who need it

Emergency Hero Protocol

When you see someone needs help:
1. Assess the situation
2. Think how you can help
3. Act without seeking credit
4. Keep it secret if possible

Victory Dance Moments □

You're winning when:
- You help without being asked
- Nobody knows your good deeds
- You make others smile
- You serve without rewards

Boss Battle Tips:

Being a real hero:
1. Look for needs

2. Act quickly
3. Stay humble
4. Keep secrets

The Ultimate Power Move

Want to be legendarily good? Be someone who:
- Helps without hesitation
- Serves without recognition
- Gives without reward
- Loves without limits

Bonus Round: Hero Stats

True heroes are:
- Quick to help
- Slow to brag
- Ready to serve
- Happy to be secret

Final Boss Thought:

The real superpower isn't doing amazing things - it's doing good things amazingly well!

The Secret Strategy Guide 📖

Ways to level up your hero status:
1. Start small
2. Stay consistent
3. Keep quiet
4. Help everyone
5. Expect nothing back

Stay heroic, stay humble, and keep spreading that goodness! #SecretHero #KindnessNinja #SpreadGood #BeTheLight

Quick Hero Ideas 💡

Try these stealth missions:
1. Clean something nobody notices
2. Leave anonymous encouragement notes
3. Do someone else's chores
4. Share your lunch with someone who forgot theirs

P.S. - Remember how Jesus said not to let your left hand know what your right hand is doing? He was basically saying "Be a stealth hero!" That's next-level awesome! 🥷

Remember: The greatest heroes aren't always wearing capes - sometimes they're just regular kids doing kind things when nobody's watching! Now go forth and be awesome! ☺

Stay epic, stay kind, and remember: Every secret good deed is leveling up your eternal character stats! 💪

#StealthKindness #SecretMissions #HeroMode #GodSquad

Chapter 16: How to Deal With People Who Drive You Crazy!

Yo future saints! Ready to learn the ultimate skill of keeping cool when others are super annoying? Let's master the art of not losing it when people get on your last nerve!

The Patience Challenge 🎯

Common Reaction Fails:

Picture that kid who:
- Explodes over tiny annoyances
- Can't handle annoying siblings
- Gets triggered by every little thing
- Holds grudges forever
- Has zero chill with difficult people

(If you're feeling attacked right now, don't worry - we're about to upgrade your patience stats! 😊)

The Epic Truth Bomb 💣

Here's the mind-blowing reality: Dealing with annoying people is like playing a game on expert mode - it's tough, but beating this level makes you super powerful!

Why Patience is Your Secret Weapon:
1. Makes you look super mature
2. Keeps you out of trouble
3. Earns respect from adults
4. Gives you inner peace powers

Action Items (Your Patience Quest):

Daily Missions:
1. Stay cool with one annoying person
2. Count to 10 when triggered
3. Find one good thing about someone difficult
4. Respond with kindness to rudeness

Boss Level Challenges:
1. Be nice to your most annoying sibling
2. Help someone who's mean to you
3. Keep calm when someone's pushing your buttons
4. Forgive someone who doesn't deserve it

The LOL Learning Moments 😂

Classic Reaction Fails:
- Screaming "I'M NOT ANGRY!" (while clearly angry)
- Door slamming championships
- Epic eye-rolling contests
- "Whatever" said in 57 different tones

Reflection Questions (Chill Check Time!):
1. Who pushes your buttons the most?
2. What's your typical reaction to annoyance?
3. How long do you stay mad?
4. What helps you calm down?

The Patience Toolbox ☐

Essential Equipment:
- Chill Pills
- Deep Breathing Power-Up
- Prayer Shield
- Peace Mode Activator

Weekly Challenge: Operation Keep Cool

This week's mission:
1. No eye rolling
2. Zero door slams
3. Respond calmly to annoyances
4. Find good in difficult people

Emergency Patience Protocol 👻

When about to lose it:
1. Take deep breaths
2. Count to 10 (or 100 if needed!)
3. Walk away if necessary
4. Remember this is temporary

Victory Dance Moments ☐

You're winning when:
- Small things don't bug you
- You stay cool under pressure
- You help others stay calm
- You're known for being patient

Boss Battle Tips:

Dealing with difficult people:
1. Remember they might be having a rough time

2. Kill them with kindness
3. Pray for them (seriously!)
4. Keep your peace

The Ultimate Power Move

Want to be legendarily patient? Be someone who:
- Stays calm in chaos
- Shows kindness to the unkind
- Forgives easily
- Keeps their cool

Bonus Round: Patience Stats

True strength shows in:
- How you handle annoyance
- What you do when provoked
- How you treat difficult people
- When you choose peace

Final Boss Thought:

Nobody can make you lose your cool without your permission! You're the player in control of your reactions!

The Secret Strategy Guide 📖

Ways to level up your patience:
1. Start with prayer
2. Practice deep breathing
3. Choose your battles
4. Find the funny
5. Remember it's temporary

Stay cool, stay kind, and keep that patience strong!

Quick Calm-Down Tricks 🎮

When triggered, try:
1. The 5-5-5 method (Breathe 5 seconds, hold 5, release 5)
2. The Name Game (Name 5 things you can see, 4 you can touch...)
3. The Peace Prayer (Quick prayer for patience)
4. The Exit Strategy (Walk away if needed)

P.S. - Remember how Jesus dealt with difficult people? He was like the ultimate patience master! When in doubt, ask yourself "What would Jesus do?" (Spoiler: Probably not throat punch them! 😊)

Remember: The most powerful people aren't those who never get annoyed - they're the ones who stay cool anyway! Now go forth and spread that chill! ☺

Stay awesome, stay patient, and remember: Every annoying person is just helping you level up your patience stats! 💪
#PatienceWarrior #KeepCool #LevelUp #InnerPeace

Chapter 17: So You Think Being Religious Makes You Boring? WRONG!

The Great "Holy vs. Fun" Myth

Hey there, future saint! Worried that being religious means turning into a walking statue who only speaks in Bible verses and never laughs? HA! Let me blow your mind!

What People Think Religious Life Is:
- Sitting quietly with a permanent serious face
- Never having fun
- Speaking only in King James English
- Being allergic to laughter
- Living in a constant state of "thou shalt not"

What It Actually Is:
- Being part of the most epic adventure ever
- Having the ultimate life guide
- Getting insider info from the Creator of the universe
- Being part of God's awesome team
- Having supernatural backup

The REAL Religious Life Challenge

Mission Objectives:
1. Be holy without being holier-than-thou
2. Have fun without being foolish
3. Be different without being weird
4. Be serious about God while seriously enjoying life

Action Time! (Because Reading Without Doing is Like Playing a Game on Pause)

Daily Quests:

☑☐ Do something fun that makes God smile ☑☐ Show someone that Christians can be cool ☑☐ Find joy in something ordinary ☑☐ Make at least one person laugh

Harder Missions:

☑☐ Be different from the crowd in a good way ☑☐ Stand up for what's right while staying likable ☑☐ Make prayer fun (yes, it's possible!) ☑☐ Turn a boring task into an adventure with God

The "Don't Be a Religious Robot" Checklist:
- Can you laugh at yourself? ☐
- Do you enjoy life? ☐
- Are you fun to be around? ☐
- Do others see joy in your faith? ☐

If you checked all boxes, congratulations! You're doing it right!

Emergency Fun Protocols:

When you're getting too serious:
1. Remember Jesus went to parties
2. Dance like David (maybe keep your clothes on though)
3. Find the funny side of life
4. Remember God invented laughter

Real Talk Time (With a Side of Giggles):

Q: "But what if I'm having too much fun?" A: Unless you're sinning or setting something on fire, you're probably fine.

Q: "Can I still play video games?" A: Yes! Just maybe not the ones that would make Jesus facepalm.

Q: "Do I have to stop telling jokes?" A: Nope! Just keep them clean enough that you wouldn't mind telling them to Jesus.

Your Weekly Mission (Should You Choose to Accept It):
1. Monday: Make someone laugh without being mean
2. Tuesday: Find joy in a boring task
3. Wednesday: Show kindness in a creative way
4. Thursday: Have fun while helping others
5. Friday: Be different in a good way
6. Saturday: Enjoy life while honoring God
7. Sunday: Worship with joy (Yes, you can smile in church!)

Final Thoughts (The Not-So-Boring Truth):

Being religious isn't about being boring - it's about being so filled with God's joy that others want what you have! It's like having the ultimate cheat code for life, but legal and ethical!

Your Call to Action (Because Reading This Isn't Enough):
1. Write down three ways you can make your faith more joyful
2. Plan one fun activity that would make God smile
3. Find a way to show others that following God isn't boring
4. Start tomorrow morning with a smile and a prayer

Remember: Jesus' first miracle was at a party (turning water into wine), so clearly, He's not against having a good time! Just keep it holy, keep it happy, and keep it real!

Now go forth and be awesomely religious - with a side of fun! ☺

P.S. - If you're not having fun following God, you might be doing it wrong. Time to level up your joy stats!

Chapter 18: Learning from the OG Saints (Without Falling Asleep!)

The "Ancient Heroes Aren't Boring" Challenge

Hey there, future champion! Think reading about old saints is as exciting as watching paint dry? WRONG! These were some of the most epic people ever - they were like the original superhero squad!

What Most People Think About Saints:
- Boring people who never smiled
- Always walking around with halos
- Never did anything fun
- Probably lived in caves eating bugs
- Spoke only in Bible verses

What They Were Actually Like:
- Ultimate rebellion leaders (against evil)

- Spiritual ninjas
- God's special forces team
- People who changed the world
- Regular humans who did extraordinary things

Action Time! (Because These Saints Didn't Just Sit Around!)
Daily Missions:
1. Learn one cool saint story
2. Try to copy one awesome saint move
3. Find a saint who dealt with your struggles
4. Make their lessons work in your life

The "Be Like a Saint Without Being Weird" Guide:
Level 1: Beginner Saint Moves
- Pray without looking bored
- Be kind when no one's watching
- Stand up for what's right
- Help others without bragging

Level 2: Advanced Saint Skills
- Face fears with faith
- Choose right when it's hard
- Stay cool when life's tough
- Love people who are annoying

Real Talk With Examples:
"But saints were perfect!" WRONG! Check these out:
- Augustine: Total party animal before conversion
- Peter: Epic fail denier, still became pope
- Paul: Used to hunt Christians, became Christianity's MVP

Your Weekly Saint Challenge:
Monday: "The Patience Test"
- Someone's annoying you? St. Francis dealt with worse!

Tuesday: "The Courage Quest"
- Scared of something? Daniel chilled with lions!

Wednesday: "The Kindness Mission"
- Be nice to someone mean (Mother Teresa style)

Thursday: "The Joy Challenge"
- Find happiness in hard times (like Paul singing in prison)

Friday: "The Stand Strong Task"

- Don't follow the crowd (like Noah building an ark with no rain)

Emergency Saint Protocols:

When life gets tough, ask yourself:
1. "What would [insert cool saint] do?"
2. "How did they handle worse situations?"
3. "What can I learn from their epic wins?"

Fun Facts That Make Saints Relatable:
- David was a shepherd boy who became king
- Matthew was a tax collector (basically everyone hated him)
- Peter was a fisherman who couldn't swim (probably)
- Joseph was the kid everyone picked on

Your Call to Action (Because Saints Didn't Just Read About Being Holy):
1. Pick a Saint to Learn About
- Choose someone who dealt with your struggles
- Read their story like it's a superhero comic
- Find out how they overcame their problems
2. Make Their Lessons Work Today
- Having trouble with studies? St. Thomas Aquinas got you
- Family drama? Joseph's got some tips
- Friend problems? Jesus handled that too
3. Start Your Own Saint Story
- Do one brave thing today
- Help someone who can't help you back
- Choose right when it's hard
- Be extraordinary in ordinary situations

The "Make It Real" Challenge:

Today's Mission:
1. Find one saint who was like you
2. Learn how they handled tough stuff
3. Try one of their strategies
4. Write down what happened

Remember: Saints weren't born with halos - they were regular people who made awesome choices! You can too!

Now go forth and be legendary! (Just maybe skip the living-in-a-cave part.) ☺

P.S. - Next time someone says saints are boring, remind them that St. Patrick drove snakes out of Ireland (which is basically like being a supernatural pest control expert)!

Extra Credit Mission: Find out which saint would make the best video game character and why! (St. George fought a dragon - just saying!)

Chapter 19: The Not-So-Boring Guide to Being a Spiritual Champion!

The "Daily Spiritual Workout" Challenge

Think being spiritually fit is all about sitting quietly with your eyes closed? HA! Let's turn your spiritual life from "snooze fest" to "epic adventure"!

What People Think Spiritual Exercise Is:
- Staring at walls
- Never having fun
- Speaking in whispers
- Being super serious all the time
- Endless boring routines

What It Actually Is:
- Training for life's boss battles
- Building your spiritual muscles
- Becoming mentally unbeatable
- Developing supernatural resilience
- Getting stronger every day

The Daily Training Program

Morning Warm-Up:
1. Prayer Push-Ups
   - Quick "Good morning, God!"
   - Three things you're thankful for
   - One person you want to help today
2. Bible Bench Press

- Read one chapter
- Find one verse that speaks to you
- Actually try to use it today

Midday Power Moves:
1. The Kindness Workout
- Hold the door for someone
- Share your snack
- Say something nice (and mean it!)
2. The Self-Control Sprint
- Don't lose your cool in traffic
- Skip the gossip session
- Choose not to complain

Action Time! (Because Couch Potato Christians Aren't a Thing)
Daily Challenges:
☑☐ Do one hard right thing ☑☐ Help someone secretly ☑☐ Practice what you preach ☑☐ Face one fear with faith

The "Am I Actually Growing?" Test:
Ask yourself:
1. "Could I handle more spiritual responsibility?"
2. "Am I stronger than last month?"
3. "Would others want my kind of faith?"
4. "Do I actually enjoy this spiritual journey?"

Emergency Spiritual Energy Boosters:
When feeling spiritually lazy:
1. Call a faith friend
2. Listen to worship music (the not-boring kind)
3. Read about someone who inspires you
4. Do something kind (it's like spiritual caffeine)

Your Weekly Training Schedule:
Monday: "The Focus Challenge"
- Actually pay attention during prayer
- Bonus points if you don't think about lunch

Tuesday: "The Service Sprint"
- Find three ways to help others
- Extra credit: Don't post about it on social media

Wednesday: "The Joy Jumps"
- Choose happiness when things go wrong

- Practice laughing at problems

Thursday: "The Forgiveness Flex"
- Let go of one grudge
- Warning: May cause inner peace

Friday: "The Faith Climb"
- Take one brave step forward
- Try not to look down

Real Talk Action Items:
1. Morning Mission:
- Wake up 10 minutes earlier
- Actually use those 10 minutes for God
- Try not to fall back asleep during prayer
2. Daily Quest:
- Find one way to show God's love
- Preferably without embarrassing yourself
- Make it genuine, make it count
3. Evening Challenge:
- Review your day with God
- Thank Him for wins
- Laugh about fails
- Plan tomorrow's adventure

The "Make It Fun" Factor:
Turn regular tasks into spiritual exercises:
- Cleaning your room? Practice gratitude
- Doing homework? Work like it's for God
- Dealing with siblings? Ultimate patience training
- Waiting in line? Perfect prayer time

Your Immediate Call to Action:
RIGHT NOW:
1. Pick one spiritual exercise to start today
2. Tell someone your plan (accountability is key!)
3. Set a reminder on your phone
4. Actually do it when the reminder goes off

Remember: Spiritual champions aren't born - they're made through daily training! Now get out there and start exercising (spiritually, that is)!

P.S. - If your spiritual life feels boring, you're probably doing it wrong. Time to switch up your routine!
Extra Credit: Try praying while doing jumping jacks. (Okay, maybe not, but getting active in your faith is the point!)

Chapter 20: The Ultimate Guide to Finding Peace When Life Is CRAZY!

The "Finding Your Chill in Chaos" Challenge
Think peace is only for monks living on mountaintops? NOPE! Let's learn how to find your zen even when life is going bonkers!

What People Think Peace Looks Like:
- Living in complete silence
- Never having problems
- Floating on clouds
- Always speaking in whispers
- Living in slow motion

What Real Peace Actually Is:
- Staying calm in a test when you forgot to study
- Not freaking out when your phone dies
- Keeping cool when siblings drive you nuts
- Being okay when plans change
- Finding quiet in the middle of chaos

The Daily Peace Practice
Morning Peace Prep:
1. The Two-Minute Quiet Time
- Find a spot where no one will bug you
- Take three deep breaths
- Think one happy thought
- Say a quick prayer (No, hiding under your bed doesn't count)
2. The Peace Protection Plan
- Plan for things that might stress you
- Have backup plans for your backup plans

- Remember: Most disasters are just inconveniences in disguise

Action Time! (Because Peace Doesn't Find You - You Find It!)
Daily Challenges:

☑☐ Stay calm when something goes wrong ☑☐ Find quiet in a noisy place ☑☐ Help someone else find peace ☑☐ Choose not to panic (even when justified)

The "Are You Actually Peaceful?" Test:
Quick Check:
1. Did you yell at anyone today?
2. How many times did you say "I can't even!"?
3. Did you roll your eyes in the last hour?
4. Are you breathing normally right now?

Emergency Peace Protocols:
When about to lose it:
1. Stop
2. Breathe
3. Count to 10
4. Ask: "Will this matter in 5 years?" (If counting to 10 isn't enough, try 100. Still not enough? Try algebra.)

Your Weekly Peace Mission:
Monday: "The Traffic Test"
- Stay calm when someone walks slowly in front of you
- Bonus points if it's a group taking up the whole hallway

Tuesday: "The Technology Trial"
- Keep cool when WiFi is slow
- Extra credit: Don't throw your device

Wednesday: "The Family Focus"
- Be patient with annoying siblings
- Remember: They're probably not actually trying to ruin your life

Thursday: "The Schedule Scramble"
- Handle changes without drama
- Practice saying "It's fine" and actually meaning it

Friday: "The Social Media Skip"
- Take a break from the drama
- Watch your peace levels rise dramatically

Real-Life Applications:
1. When Your Phone Dies:
   - Remember it's not actually the end of the world
   - Use this as forced peaceful time
   - Pretend you're in the 1800s (they survived!)
2. During Tests:
   - Breathe deeply
   - Remember: This test isn't your whole life
   - Channel your inner peaceful warrior
3. With Family:
   - Create a personal quiet signal
   - Find your happy place
   - Remember you actually love them (most of the time)

Your Immediate Peace Mission:
RIGHT NOW:
1. Find something that's bugging you
2. Choose to let it go
3. Feel the peace flow
4. Resist the urge to tell everyone how peaceful you are

Remember: Peace isn't the absence of chaos - it's staying calm in the middle of it!

Bonus Peace Points:
Try these when life gets extra:
- Count backward from 100 (in Spanish for extra distraction)
- Name all 50 states (geography and peace combined!)
- List your favorite pizza toppings
- Think about puppies (works every time)

P.S. - If finding peace was easy, everyone would be walking around like zen masters. It takes practice, but you've got this!

Extra Challenge: Try to stay peaceful while someone eats chips loudly near you. (Now THAT'S advanced level peace!)

Remember: You can't control the chaos around you, but you can control your response to it. Choose peace! (And maybe invest in some noise-canceling headphones.) ☺

Chapter 21: The Heart Check: When Your Feelings Feel Like a Roller Coaster!

The "Getting Your Heart Right" Challenge

Think having a good heart means being a softie? WRONG! Let's learn how to have a heart that's both strong AND good!

What People Think Having Heart Means:
- Crying at every puppy video
- Never getting mad at anything
- Being everyone's emotional sponge
- Writing poetry about flowers
- Hugging trees (not that there's anything wrong with that)

What It Actually Means:
- Being brave when scared
- Staying kind when others aren't
- Doing right when feeling wrong
- Having strength AND compassion
- Being tough AND tender

The Daily Heart Workout

Morning Heart Check:
1. The Quick Scan
- How's your attitude today?
- Anyone you need to forgive?
- Are you carrying any grudges? (If yes, drop them - they're too heavy!)
2. The Heart Reset
- Think one grateful thought
- Plan one kind action
- Choose joy (even if you don't feel like it)

Action Time! (Because Feelings Follow Actions)

Daily Heart Challenges:

☑☐ Do something kind when you're grumpy ☑☐ Forgive someone who doesn't deserve it ☑☐ Choose joy in an annoying situation ☑☐ Be brave when you want to run

The "How's Your Heart?" Test:

Quick Questions:

1. Can you laugh at yourself?
2. Do you want others to succeed?
3. Are you holding any grudges?
4. Would others say you're kind?

Emergency Heart Protocols:
When your heart's not in the right place:
1. Stop the grump train
2. Remember who you want to be
3. Do something kind
4. Repeat until attitude improves (Warning: May result in accidental happiness)

Your Weekly Heart Goals:
Monday: "The Forgiveness Challenge"
- Let go of one tiny grudge
- Your blood pressure will thank you

Tuesday: "The Joy Journey"
- Find happiness in three annoying things
- Yes, even in math class

Wednesday: "The Kindness Quest"
- Be nice to someone who's not
- Watch their confusion - it's entertaining!

Thursday: "The Gratitude Game"
- List 5 good things about your worst subject
- Being creative counts!

Friday: "The Peace Project"
- Choose calm in chaos
- Pretend you're a zen master (results may vary)

Real-Life Applications:
1. When Someone's Mean:
- Remember they might be having a rough day
- Kill them with kindness
- Watch them malfunction in confusion
2. When You're Frustrated:
- Take three deep breaths
- Think about pizza
- Remember this too shall pass
3. When Everything's Wrong:

- Find one right thing
- Focus on that
- Build from there

Your Immediate Heart Mission:
RIGHT NOW:
1. Find one thing that's bugging you
2. Choose to change your heart about it
3. Take one positive action
4. Notice how much better you feel

Remember: Your heart follows your actions. Act right, feel right!

Bonus Heart Points:
Try these heart exercises:
- Write a thank you note to someone annoying
- Find good in your least favorite person
- Pray for someone who bugs you (Warning: They might actually become likeable!)

The Ultimate Heart Challenge:
Can you:
- Stay kind when others are mean?
- Keep calm when everything's crazy?
- Choose joy when things are tough?
- Be brave when you're scared?

P.S. - Having a good heart doesn't mean being weak - it means being strong enough to stay good when it's hard!

Extra Credit: Try being happy during Monday morning math class. (Now THAT'S a superpower!)

Remember: Your heart is like a garden - what you plant is what grows. Plant good stuff! (And maybe some actual plants too, if you're into that.) ☺

Chapter 22: The Ultimate Guide to Handling Life's Epic Fails!

The "When Everything Goes Wrong" Survival Guide

Think you're the only one who messes up? HA! Let's learn how to bounce back when life throws you a curveball (or several)!

What People Think Misery Is:
- Getting a B+ instead of an A
- Bad hair day
- Phone battery at 1%
- No WiFi for an hour
- Someone ate your last cookie

What Real Challenges Look Like:
- Actually failing a test
- Major embarrassments
- Real disappointments
- Tough family stuff
- True friend drama

The Recovery Plan

Immediate Response Protocol:
1. The Quick Check
   - Is anyone bleeding? No?
   - Will this matter in 5 years?
   - Can it be fixed?
   - Would this make a funny story later?
2. The Bounce-Back Strategy
   - Take three deep breaths
   - Remember past victories
   - Make a comeback plan
   - Find the lesson (there's always one hiding)

Action Time! (Because Wallowing Is Not A Sport)

Emergency Recovery Steps:

☑☐ Admit what went wrong ☑☐ Find the funny part ☑☐ Make a fix-it plan ☑☐ Learn something useful (Note: Crying in your pillow for 5 minutes is allowed, but set a timer!)

The "It's Not The End of The World" Test:

Ask yourself:

1. Will anyone remember this next month?
   2. Can you turn this into a good story?
   3. What's the worst that could happen?
   4. What's the best that could come from this?

Emergency Fail Protocols:
When disaster strikes:
   1. Don't panic (panic helps nothing)
   2. Find perspective (it's probably not that bad)
   3. Make a plan (any plan is better than no plan)
   4. Take action (sitting and sulking doesn't fix anything)

Your Comeback Strategy:
Step 1: "The Reality Check"
   - Rate your disaster on a scale of 1-10
   - Subtract 5 points (we always exaggerate)

Step 2: "The Solution Sprint"
   - List three possible fixes
   - Pick the least dramatic one

Step 3: "The Growth Goal"
   - Find one lesson in this mess
   - Plan how to avoid repeat fails

Real-Life Applications:
   1. Failed a Test:
   - Remember Einstein probably failed something too
   - Make a study plan
   - Actually use the study plan (that's the hard part)
   2. Social Disaster:
   - Remember everyone's too busy thinking about themselves
   - Tomorrow will bring new drama
   - This will be funny... eventually
   3. Family Problems:
   - Take the high road
   - Be the bigger person
   - Remember they're stuck with you anyway

Your Immediate Recovery Mission:
RIGHT NOW:
   1. Name your current disaster

2. Rate it realistically
3. Find one funny thing about it
4. Make one small plan to fix it

The Ultimate Perspective Shift:
Remember:
- Every hero has failed
- Every success story includes mistakes
- Every expert started as a beginner
- Every "overnight success" took years

Bonus Recovery Points:
Try these comeback moves:
- Tell your fail story first (before others do)
- Find someone who failed bigger
- Plan your epic comeback
- Write your future success story

The Final Truth:
It's not about how many times you fall, it's about:
- How many times you get back up
- What you learn while you're down there
- How you help others up later
- Whether you can laugh about it eventually

P.S. - If you haven't failed at anything lately, you're probably not trying hard enough!

Extra Challenge: Try to fail at something small on purpose, just to practice recovering. (But maybe not during an actual test.) ☺

Remember: Today's epic fail is tomorrow's funny story. Make it a good one! Just maybe leave out the really embarrassing parts when you tell it later... ☺

Chapter 23: The Not-So-Fun Guide to Thinking About Death (But We'll Make It Interesting!)

The "Let's Talk About The Unavoidable" Challenge
Think death is too depressing to think about? Actually, understanding it makes life WAY more meaningful! Let's dive in (without getting too dark)!

What People Avoid Thinking About:
- The limited time we have
- The importance of each day
- The things that really matter
- The legacy we'll leave
- The eternal stuff

What Smart People Think About:
- Making each day count
- Building something lasting
- Living with no regrets
- Creating good memories
- Preparing for eternity

The Daily Life Check
Morning Reality Boost:
1. The Quick Questions
- What would I do if this was my last year?
- Am I spending time on what matters?
- Would I be proud of today's choices? (No pressure, but also... yes pressure!)
2. The Life Maximizer
- Plan one meaningful action
- Tell someone you love them
- Do something that lasts

Action Time! (Because YOLO Actually Means Something)
Daily Purpose Challenges:
☑☐ Do one thing future-you would thank you for ☑☐ Create one good memory ☑☐ Help someone in a lasting way ☑☐ Build something meaningful

The "Am I Living Well?" Test:

Quick Check:
1. Would you be proud of today?
2. Are you avoiding important things?
3. Have you told people you care?
4. Are you ready for anything?

Life Maximizing Protocols:
For making life count:
1. Stop wasting time on dumb stuff
2. Start doing what matters
3. Tell people you love them NOW
4. Build something lasting (Note: Building a massive pizza fort doesn't count as "lasting")

Your Weekly Life Mission:
Monday: "The Legacy Launch"
- Do something people will remember well
- Preferably legal and kind

Tuesday: "The Relationship Builder"
- Strengthen one important relationship
- Actually talk to family members (yes, really)

Wednesday: "The Impact Investment"
- Help someone in a meaningful way
- Create something that lasts

Thursday: "The Eternal Perspective"
- Focus on what really matters
- Skip the temporary drama

Friday: "The Memory Maker"
- Create one awesome memory
- Make it Instagram-worthy (but maybe don't post it)

Real Applications:
1. With Family:
- Say the important stuff
- Spend real time together
- Take the photos
- Make the memories
2. With Friends:
- Have the real talks
- Be the good influence

- Create the adventures
- Share the love
3. With Time:
- Use it wisely
- Don't waste it
- Make it count
- Fill it with good

Your Immediate Life Mission:
RIGHT NOW:
1. Text someone you love
2. Plan one meaningful action
3. Start something lasting
4. Live today on purpose

The Ultimate Life Challenge:
Ask yourself:
- What do I want to be remembered for?
- What am I building that lasts?
- Who am I helping?
- What's my legacy?

Final Perspective:
Life is like a video game with:
- Limited play time
- No save points
- No restarts
- High stakes
- Eternal consequences

P.S. - This isn't meant to be depressing - it's meant to make you awesome! Live like you mean it!

Extra Challenge: Write your future biography. Make it epic. Then start living it!

Remember: Life is short, but it's the longest thing you'll do on Earth. Make it count! And yes, eating dessert first sometimes is totally valid life strategy. ☺

Chapter 24: The Epic Guide to Not Freaking Out About Judgment Day!

The "Final Boss Battle" Preparation Guide

Think judgment is just for courtroom TV shows? Think again! Let's get ready for the ultimate performance review (without having a panic attack)!

What People Think Judgment Is:
- Getting busted for stealing cookies
- Having Mom find your hidden phone
- Teacher catching you not paying attention
- Principal seeing you run in halls
- Dad checking your browser history

What It Actually Is:
- The ultimate life review
- The final score check
- The real report card
- The eternal consequence counter
- The ultimate truth reveal

The Life Audit Prep

Daily Readiness Check:
1. The Quick Scan
- Would I be okay if today was the day?
- Are there things I need to fix?
- Have I helped or hurt others?
- What's my current score? (Spoiler: We all need improvement!)
2. The Reality Alignments
- Fix one wrong thing
- Help one person
- Make one good choice
- Create one positive impact

Action Time! (Because "Later" Might Be Too Late)

Daily Preparation Tasks:

☑☐ Clean up one mess (literal or metaphorical) ☑☐ Fix one relationship ☑☐ Right one wrong ☑☐ Add one good deed to your eternal resume

The "Am I Ready?" Test:
Quick Check:
1. Any unfixed mistakes?
2. Outstanding apologies needed?
3. Unfinished good deeds?
4. Hidden report card under your bed? (Okay, that last one isn't eternal, but Mom might disagree)

Emergency Preparation Protocols:
When reality hits:
1. Don't panic (panic cleaning doesn't work)
2. Start with what's fixable
3. Do what you can now
4. Trust God's mercy (He's strict but fair, and thankfully, very forgiving!)

Your Weekly Readiness Plan:
Monday: "The Truth Check"
- Be honest about where you stand
- Make one improvement (No, cleaning your room doesn't count... but maybe do that too)

Tuesday: "The Relationship Repair"
- Fix one broken friendship
- Apologize if needed (Even if it wasn't TOTALLY your fault)

Wednesday: "The Good Deed Derby"
- Help someone who can't repay you
- Be kind when no one's watching (Yes, being nice to siblings counts double)

Thursday: "The Eternal Investment"
- Do something with lasting value
- Build something good (TikTok followers don't count as lasting value)

Real-Life Applications:
1. At Home:
- Be the good kid your mom brags about
- Help without being asked
- Tell the truth (even about the broken vase)
2. At School:

- Be kind to the uncool kids
- Help others succeed
- Do your own homework (Copying isn't an eternal strategy)

Your Immediate Mission:
RIGHT NOW:
1. Fix one wrong thing
2. Help one person
3. Make one good choice
4. Start one positive habit

Remember: The final judgment isn't about being perfect - it's about trying your best and trusting God's grace!

The Ultimate Preparation Guide:
Think of life like a video game where:
- Every choice matters
- Good deeds are power-ups
- Kindness gives bonus points
- Love is the highest score
- Grace is the cheat code (but you still have to play well!)

P.S. - Don't wait to be good! Start now! (But also maybe clean your room - seriously, what IS that growing under your bed?)

Extra Challenge: Live today like someone's watching... because Someone is! ☺

Remember: The best way to prepare for judgment isn't to fear it - it's to live so well you look forward to your review! (And maybe keep your room clean... just saying!)

Chapter 25: The Epic Makeover Guide: How to Level Up Your ENTIRE Life!

The "Total Life Upgrade" Challenge

Think changing your life requires moving to a monastery or becoming a TikTok influencer? NOPE! Let's make some real changes that don't involve becoming a monk or getting famous!

What People THINK Life Change Looks Like:
- Dramatic hair dye moments
- Buying entirely new wardrobes
- Moving to a different country
- Becoming a completely different person overnight
- Getting bitten by a radioactive spider

What REAL Change Actually Is:
- Making your bed (yes, really!)
- Doing homework BEFORE dinner
- Being nice to your siblings (the ultimate challenge)
- Actually listening when others talk
- Choosing water instead of soda (sometimes)

The Daily Upgrade Plan

Morning Revolution:
1. The "New You" Checklist
- Wake up 10 minutes earlier
- Make your bed (Mom will faint)
- Plan one good deed
- Choose joy (even on Mondays)
2. The Quick Wins
- Drink water first thing
- Say something nice to family
- Plan your attack on the day (Note: Real attacks not recommended)

Action Time! (Because Reading Without Doing is Just Napping with Your Eyes Open)

Today's Missions:

☑☐ Fix ONE small bad habit ☑☐ Start ONE good habit ☑☐ Clean ONE thing ☑☐ Help ONE person (See? No monastery required!)

The "Am I Actually Changing?" Test:
Ask yourself:
1. Did I level up in any way today?
2. Would my future self thank me?
3. Did I surprise my parents (in a good way)?
4. Am I better than yesterday?

Emergency Change Protocols:
When motivation dies:
1. Do the smallest possible good thing
2. Celebrate like you won an Olympic medal
3. Build on that tiny victory
4. Repeat until awesome

Your Weekly Challenge Ladder:
Monday: "The Attitude Adjustment"
- Smile before noon
- Don't complain for 24 hours (Harder than it sounds!)

Tuesday: "The Habit Upgrade"
- Replace ONE bad habit with good
- Example: Switch video games for book (Comic books totally count)

Wednesday: "The Kindness Revolution"
- Help someone unexpectedly
- Be nice to an annoying person (Yes, even THAT person)

Practical Action Steps:
1. Right Now:
- Clean one thing
- Fix one small thing
- Plan one improvement
- Do one push-up (Okay, maybe five push-ups)
2. Today:
- Drink more water
- Eat one vegetable
- Thank someone
- Read something useful (Social media doesn't count!)
3. This Week:
- Fix one relationship
- Learn one new skill

- Create one good habit
- Break one bad habit

The Ultimate Change Challenge:

Can you:
- Go one day without complaining?
- Help without being asked?
- Do homework without reminders?
- Be nice to siblings ALL DAY? (We believe in you!)

Your Immediate Mission:

STOP READING AND:
1. Clean something small
2. Fix something broken
3. Help someone nearby
4. Start one good habit (No, planning to start tomorrow doesn't count!)

Remember: Real change is like building with LEGOs - one piece at a time makes something awesome!

P.S. - If changing yourself was easy, everyone would be perfect. Start small, stay consistent, become legendary!

Extra Credit: Try explaining to your parents why you're suddenly being so helpful without making them suspicious! 😊

Now go forth and upgrade your life! Just remember: No capes. They're impractical and get caught in doors. Trust me on this one.

Chapter 26: How to Level Up Your Prayer Game (Without Falling Asleep!)

The "Make Prayer Actually Awesome" Challenge

Think prayer is just boring mumbling while trying not to doze off? NOPE! Let's turn your prayer life from snooze fest to power session!

What People THINK Prayer Looks Like:
- Kneeling for hours until your legs go numb
- Speaking in thee's and thou's
- Staring at ceiling while mind wanders
- Falling asleep mid-sentence
- Reciting boring memorized stuff

What REAL Prayer Can Be:
- Having an actual conversation with God
- Being real about your day
- Sharing your epic wins and fails
- Getting supernatural backup
- Divine life coaching sessions

The Daily Prayer Revolution

Morning Power-Up:
1. The Quick Connect
- "Hey God, let's rock this day!"
- Share your biggest worry
- Ask for one specific thing
- Thank Him for something good
2. The Action Prayer
- Pray while making your bed
- Talk to God during breakfast
- Have prayer thoughts in shower (Just don't get so distracted you use shampoo twice)

Action Time! (Because Prayer Without Action is Just Wishful Thinking)

Today's Prayer Missions:

☑☐ Have ONE real conversation with God ☑☐ Pray for someone else (not just yourself!) ☑☐ Thank God for three specific things ☑☐ Ask for help with one challenge

The "Is My Prayer Life Awake?" Test:
Quick Check:
1. Did you pray without falling asleep?
2. Can you remember what you prayed about?
3. Did you pray beyond "help me pass this test"?
4. Were you real with God?

Emergency Prayer Protocols:
When prayer feels boring:
1. Switch locations (try praying outside)
2. Move around (prayer walks are cool)
3. Write it down (prayer journaling)
4. Use normal words (God understands teen language)

Your Weekly Prayer Challenge:
Monday: "The Gratitude Game"
- List 10 things you're thankful for
- No repeating "pizza" ten times

Tuesday: "The Others Focus"
- Pray for five friends
- Include that one annoying person (Yes, that one. God loves them too!)

Wednesday: "The Real Talk"
- Share your actual feelings with God
- He can handle your honesty (Even about that math test)

Practical Prayer Steps:
1. Right Now:
- Say a 30-second prayer
- Use your own words
- Be completely honest
- Thank God for something
2. Today:
- Pray during transitions
- Walking to class? Pray!
- Waiting in line? Pray!
- Stuck in traffic? Perfect prayer time!
3. This Week:
- Create a prayer playlist
- Find your prayer spot

- Start a prayer journal
- Get a prayer buddy

The Ultimate Prayer Challenge:

Try these power moves:
- Pray while exercising
- Have a prayer walk
- Create prayer art
- Make a prayer playlist (Warning: May result in actual spiritual growth!)

Your Immediate Mission:

STOP READING AND:
1. Say one honest prayer
2. Thank God for something specific
3. Pray for someone else
4. Ask for help with one thing

Remember: Prayer is just talking to God. No fancy words required. He's like your cosmic best friend who actually has the power to help!

P.S. - If your prayers are boring, you're probably doing it wrong. God invented fun - He can handle your personality!

Extra Credit: Try praying out loud while alone in your room. Just warn your family first so they don't think you're going crazy! 😁

Now go forth and revolutionize your prayer life! And remember: God's always online, never needs charging, and has unlimited data! 🐶

Chapter 27: How to Stop Being Obsessed with Yourself (Without Having an Identity Crisis!)

The "It's Not All About Me" Challenge
Think self-love means posting 47 selfies a day? NOPE! Let's learn how to get over ourselves without losing ourselves!

What People THINK Self-Focus Looks Like:
- Checking every reflective surface
- Making every story about you
- Posting your entire life online
- Being the main character in everyone's story
- Having personal theme music playing everywhere

What REAL Balance Actually Is:
- Caring about others' stories
- Making room for other people to shine
- Being awesome without announcing it
- Helping without posting about it
- Living life without a soundtrack

The Daily "Get Over Yourself" Plan
Morning Reality Check:
1. The Quick Self-Test
- How many selfies yesterday?
- Did every story start with "I"?
- When's the last time you asked about someone else?
- Are you the star of your own reality show?
2. The Balance Builder
- Plan to make someone else's day
- Choose to be the supporting actor
- Look for ways to highlight others (Warning: May result in actual friendships!)

Action Time! (Because Life Isn't Your Personal Movie)
Today's Missions:
☑☐ Make someone else the star ☑☐ Listen without waiting to talk ☑☐ Help without posting about it ☑☐ Care about someone else's story

The "Am I Too Self-Focused?" Test:

Quick Check:
1. Do you know what's happening in others' lives?
2. Can you go an hour without a selfie?
3. Do you remember others' birthdays?
4. Can you celebrate others' wins?

Emergency Self-Check Protocols:
When you're being too self-focused:
1. Ask someone about their day
2. Do something nice anonymously
3. Let someone else talk
4. Don't post about it (Yes, unposted good deeds still count!)

Your Weekly Challenge:
Monday: "The Spotlight Switch"
- Make someone else feel special
- No, not by comparing them to you

Tuesday: "The Silent Service"
- Help someone secretly
- Resist urge to reveal yourself

Wednesday: "The Story Switch"
- Let others tell their stories
- Don't hijack with your "similar" story

Practical Steps:
1. Right Now:
- Text someone asking about THEIR day
- Like posts without posting yourself
- Plan one anonymous good deed
- Delete that selfie (you know which one)
2. Today:
- Count others' words vs yours
- Make eye contact when listening
- Ask follow-up questions
- Care about answers
3. This Week:
- Go one day without posting about yourself
- Do three unannounced good deeds
- Learn five new things about friends

- Let others shine

The Ultimate Challenge:

Try to:
- Have a conversation without saying "I"
- Help without evidence
- Win without announcing
- Care without credit (Harder than it sounds!)

Your Immediate Mission:

STOP READING AND:
1. Text someone asking about THEM
2. Plan one anonymous good deed
3. Delete one "look at me" post
4. Make room for someone else to shine

Remember: You're still special, you just don't need to announce it every five minutes!

P.S. - The world is like a selfie - better when it's not all about you!

Extra Credit: Try going a whole day without posting about yourself. Yes, your followers will survive! 😁

Now go forth and be awesome... quietly! And remember: Not everything needs to be on your story. Some things can just be, you know, LIFE! ✸

#UnpostableGoodDeeds #SilentAwesome #NotAboutMe (Okay, that was the last hashtag, I promise!)

Chapter 28: How to Handle Haters (Without Becoming One Yourself!)

The "When People Are Being Sus" Challenge
Think dealing with haters means becoming a superhero or going into witness protection? NOPE! Let's learn how to handle the hate while staying awesome!

What People THINK Handling Haters Means:
- Planning elaborate revenge
- Writing angry poems in your diary
- Becoming a ninja overnight
- Moving to a different planet
- Developing superpowers

What it ACTUALLY Means:
- Staying cool when others aren't
- Living your best life anyway
- Turning haters into motivators
- Being awesome without being mean
- Rising above the drama

The Daily Anti-Hater Strategy
Morning Prep:
1. The Quick Shield Check
- Got your confidence ready?
- Remembered you're awesome?
- Prepared your comeback smile?
- Packed your "whatever" shrug?
2. The Power Moves
- Plan to kill them with kindness
- Schedule some success
- Arrange to be awesome (Success is the best revenge, but keep it classy!)

Action Time! (Because Sitting Around Being Sad Helps Nobody)
Today's Missions:
☑☐ Do one thing that makes you happy ☑☐ Succeed at something small ☑☐ Help someone (even a hater) ☑☐ Practice your unbothered face

The "Am I Handling This Right?" Test:

Quick Check:
1. Are you still being kind?
2. Have you stayed classy?
3. Are you focusing on yourself?
4. Would your grandma be proud?

Emergency Hater Protocols:
When the hate gets real:
1. Take deep breaths
2. Remember your worth
3. Do something awesome
4. Stay positive (Note: Eye rolls are permitted, but keep them subtle)

Your Weekly Victory Plan:
Monday: "The Unbothered Boss"
- Practice your "I'm too blessed to be stressed" face
- Perfect your "succeeding anyway" walk

Tuesday: "The Kind Warrior"
- Be nice to someone who isn't
- Watch their confusion (It's hilarious when they can't figure out why you're nice)

Wednesday: "The Success Strategy"
- Focus on your goals
- Let your achievements do the talking

Practical Defense Moves:
1. Right Now:
- List three things you're good at
- Plan one success
- Schedule some awesome
- Practice your victory smile
2. Today:
- Do something you love
- Succeed at something small
- Help someone else
- Stay positive
3. This Week:
- Collect some wins
- Build your confidence

- Make new friends
- Rise above drama

The Ultimate Power Move:
Try to:
- Succeed without bragging
- Win without rubbing it in
- Help those who hate
- Stay kind when others aren't (Pro level: Actually mean it!)

Your Immediate Mission:
STOP READING AND:
1. Do one thing that makes you happy
2. Plan one success
3. Help someone unexpected
4. Practice your peace

Remember: The best way to handle haters is to be so busy being awesome you forget they exist!

P.S. - Living well really is the best revenge. Plus, it's way more fun than being mad!

Extra Credit: Try being so successful and happy that your haters become your secret fans! 😎

Now go forth and be amazing! And remember: Haters are just fans in denial - they're watching you succeed, so give them a good show! ✨

Final Tip: Keep some emergency chocolate handy. It won't solve your problems, but it makes dealing with them more enjoyable! 🍫

Chapter 29: How to Stay Cool When Life Feels Like a Dumpster Fire!

The "Everything's Going Wrong But I'm Still Awesome" Challenge

Think dealing with troubles means becoming an emotional wreck or moving to a cave? NOPE! Let's learn how to handle life's chaos like a boss!

What People THINK Handling Trouble Means:
- Crying in your pillow forever
- Becoming a hermit
- Playing sad songs on repeat
- Eating ALL the ice cream
- Texting your ex (Don't. Just don't.)

What it ACTUALLY Means:
- Staying cool in the chaos
- Finding funny in the failures
- Making comebacks from crashes
- Learning from the losses
- Becoming stronger through struggles

The Daily Trouble-Busting Plan

Morning Mental Prep:
1. The Quick Strength Check
- Got your game face on?
- Remembered past victories?
- Ready to tackle problems?
- Packed your emergency snacks?
2. The Power Moves
- Plan your comeback strategy
- Schedule some small wins
- Arrange your support squad (Note: Your cat counts as emotional support)

Action Time! (Because Problems Don't Fix Themselves)

Today's Missions:

☑ Solve one small problem ☑ Find humor in one situation ☑ Help someone else (yes, while YOU'RE struggling) ☑ Create one tiny victory

The "Am I Handling This Like a Champ?" Test:
Quick Check:
1. Still breathing? (Important first step!)
2. Made any progress today?
3. Helped anyone else?
4. Found anything to smile about?

Emergency Trouble Protocols:
When it all hits the fan:
1. Don't panic (panic helps nothing)
2. Take deep breaths
3. Make a simple plan
4. Take one small action (Note: Screaming into your pillow is allowed, but set a timer)

Your Weekly Survival Guide:
Monday: "The Comeback King/Queen"
- Start small comeback plans
- Perfect your "I got this" face (Even if you don't got this yet)

Tuesday: "The Problem Solver"
- Fix one tiny thing
- Celebrate like you solved world peace

Wednesday: "The Joy Finder"
- List three good things
- Find humor in one bad thing (There's ALWAYS something funny)

Practical Survival Moves:
1. Right Now:
- Fix something small
- Help someone else
- Find one good thing
- Take one positive action
2. Today:
- Make progress on one problem
- Find something to laugh about
- Create one small victory
- Thank someone who helps
3. This Week:

- Build your support squad
- Learn from challenges
- Plan future victories
- Collect some wins

The Ultimate Power Move:
Try to:
- Stay positive in problems
- Help others while hurting
- Find humor in hard times
- Make progress despite pain (Warning: May result in actual personal growth!)

Your Immediate Mission:
STOP READING AND:
1. Fix one tiny problem
2. Help someone else
3. Find something funny
4. Take one step forward

Remember: Life's tough times are just plot twists in your awesome story!

Extra Credit: Try explaining your problems to your pet - their confused face will definitely make you laugh! 😺

P.S. - Keep emergency chocolate hidden somewhere. Future you will thank you when things get rough!

Final Tip: When life gives you lemons, make lemonade. When life gives you too many lemons, start a lemonade business. When life keeps giving you lemons, learn to juggle them! 🍋

Now go forth and conquer those troubles! And remember: Every problem is temporary, but your awesomeness is forever! 💪

Chapter 30: How to Get God's Help Without Looking Desperate!

The "Getting Divine Backup" Challenge
Think asking for God's help is like begging your parents for money? NOPE! Let's learn how to get heavenly support with style!

What People THINK Asking God Means:
- Only praying when you're failing tests
- Making deals you won't keep
- Promising to be perfect forever
- Bargaining like a used car salesman
- Emergency room-style begging

What it ACTUALLY Means:
- Having regular God-chats
- Being real about your needs
- Building actual trust
- Making legit changes
- Getting supernatural help

The Daily Divine Connection Plan
Morning Setup:
1. The Quick Connect
   - Say hi to God (He's already up!)
   - Share your actual plans
   - Ask for specific help
   - Be real about your mess
2. The Power Moves
   - Plan time with God
   - Schedule mini-prayers
   - Arrange quiet moments (No, sleeping in class doesn't count as meditation)

Action Time! (Because Faith Without Action is Just Wishful Thinking)
Today's Missions:
☑☐ Have one honest God-chat ☑☐ Ask for help with something specific ☑☐ Thank Him for something ☑☐ Take one step of faith

The "Am I Doing This Right?" Test:
Quick Check:
1. Been real with God today?
2. Asked for what you actually need?
3. Listened for answers?
4. Taken any action?

Emergency Help Protocols:
When you really need backup:
1. Send up the SOS prayer
2. Be specific about needs
3. Listen for guidance
4. Take action (Note: God helps those who help themselves... and sometimes those who just need help!)

Your Weekly Connection Plan:
Monday: "The Real Talk"
- Tell God your actual problems
- No fancy words needed (He invented slang, He can handle yours)

Tuesday: "The Trust Builder"
- Take one step of faith
- Watch for God's response

Wednesday: "The Action Partner"
- Ask for help AND take action
- Team up with the Big Guy

Practical Faith Steps:
1. Right Now:
- Say a quick prayer
- Ask for one specific thing
- Thank God for something
- Take one faith step
2. Today:
- Have three God check-ins
- Watch for answers
- Follow through on guidance
- Stay connected
3. This Week:

- Build prayer habits
- Notice God's help
- Keep it real
- Take action

The Ultimate Faith Move:
Try to:
- Trust before seeing results
- Thank God in advance
- Follow through on guidance
- Stay faithful in small things (Warning: May result in actual miracles!)

Your Immediate Mission:
STOP READING AND:
1. Say one honest prayer
2. Ask for specific help
3. Thank God for something
4. Take one faith step

Remember: God's not your emergency contact - He's your daily support system!

Extra Credit: Try praying while doing normal stuff. Walking, eating, homework (especially math - we all need divine help there!) 📚

P.S. - God's always online, never sleeps, and has unlimited data. Best support system ever!

Final Tip: Think of God like your spiritual WiFi - the connection works best when you stay in range and check in regularly! 📶

Now go forth and get that divine backup! And remember: You're not bothering God - He literally made the universe, He can handle your algebra problems! 🌀

Chapter 31: How to Focus on God When Everything's Distracting!

The "Stop Getting Distracted By Everything" Challenge

Think focusing on God is impossible when your phone keeps buzzing? Think focusing requires becoming a monk? NOPE! Let's learn how to tune in to God while living in the real world!

What People THINK Focus Means:
- Staring at clouds for hours
- Deleting all your social media
- Moving to a mountain cave
- Never looking at screens again
- Becoming allergic to fun

What it ACTUALLY Means:
- Finding God in normal stuff
- Making room for what matters
- Using technology wisely
- Having fun with faith
- Living in balance

The Daily Focus Plan

Morning Setup:
1. The Quick Focus Check
   - Is your phone really your best friend?
   - When's the last time you looked up?
   - Can you sit still for 5 minutes?
   - Do you remember what silence sounds like? (No, the sound of your game loading doesn't count)
2. The Power Moves
   - Start with 5 minutes of quiet
   - Schedule God-time like you schedule Netflix
   - Make holy habits fun (Yes, you can pray while playing sports!)

Action Time! (Because Reading This While Scrolling TikTok Doesn't Count)

Today's Missions:

☑☐ Have one distraction-free God moment ☑☐ Look up from your phone 10 times ☑☐ Find God in three normal things ☑☐ Create one focused moment

Emergency Focus Protocols:
When distractions attack:
1. Put the phone DOWN
2. Take three deep breaths
3. Look at something real
4. Remember what matters (Note: Your Snapchat streak isn't eternal)

Your Weekly Focus Challenge:
Monday: "The Tech Break"
- Go phone-free for one hour
- Survive without checking likes (You can do it! We believe in you!)

Tuesday: "The God Hunt"
- Find God in everyday stuff
- Look for holy moments in normal life (Even in math class - God's everywhere!)

Wednesday: "The Focus Builder"
- Increase attention span
- Start with 5 minutes, build up (Like working out, but for your soul)

Practical Focus Steps:
1. Right Now:
- Turn off notifications
- Look up from screen
- Notice something real
- Thank God for it
2. Today:
- Set phone-free times
- Create quiet moments
- Find God everywhere
- Make focus fun
3. This Week:
- Build attention muscle
- Reduce distractions

- Increase God-awareness
- Make it stick

The Ultimate Focus Move:
Try to:
- Pray while gaming (seriously!)
- Find God in movies
- Make faith relevant
- Turn distractions into devotions (Warning: May actually make faith fun!)

Your Immediate Mission:
STOP READING AND:
1. Put down your phone
2. Look at something real
3. Find God in it
4. Stay present for 5 minutes

Remember: God's not boring - we just need to tune in better!
Extra Credit: Try explaining to your friends why you're randomly staring at trees and smiling. (It's about finding God in nature, but they might think you're weird!) 📱
P.S. - If Jesus had a phone, He'd probably use it wisely... and have the best Instagram stories ever! 📱
Final Tip: Think of distractions like pop-up ads in life - you can click away and focus on what matters! ⚡
Now go forth and focus! And remember: Your attention span might be short, but God's patience is eternal! 🙌

CopyRetry

L

rewrite NEXT CHAPTER. make sure it is funny and actionable
Edit

Chapter 32: How to Stop Being Your Own Worst Enemy! 🚫
The "Stop Getting in Your Own Way" Challenge

Think self-denial means never having fun again? Think beating yourself up helps? NOPE! Let's learn how to get out of your own way without becoming a boring zombie!

What People THINK Self-Denial Means:
- Never eating pizza again
- Deleting all your games

- Living in eternal boredom
- Wearing only beige
- Becoming allergic to happiness

What it ACTUALLY Means:
- Being your own best teammate
- Making smart choices
- Leveling up your life
- Having better self-control
- Becoming actually awesome

The Daily Self-Control Plan
Morning Setup:
1. The Quick Self-Check
- Are you sabotaging yourself?
- Making excuses again?
- Letting your lazy side win?
- Being your own hater? (Note: Your bed is not your best friend)
2. The Power Moves
- Plan one wise choice
- Schedule one small win
- Arrange one victory (Yes, getting up counts as a victory!)

Action Time! (Because Thinking About It Isn't Doing It)
Today's Missions:
☑☐ Make one smart choice ☑☐ Say no to one temptation ☑☐ Do one hard right thing ☑☐ Choose long-term over short-term

Emergency Self-Control Protocols:
When temptation attacks:
1. Stop and think
2. Remember your goals
3. Make the smart choice
4. Reward good decisions (Note: Rewarding yourself with what you just denied defeats the purpose!)

Your Weekly Control Challenge:
Monday: "The Smart Choice"
- Choose homework over TikTok

- Survive without immediate gratification (You can watch those cat videos AFTER)

Tuesday: "The Victory Builder"
- Make three wise decisions
- Celebrate small wins (No, celebrating with cake isn't the point)

Wednesday: "The Self-Master"
- Control one bad habit
- Build one good one (Start small - maybe not eating ALL the cookies)

Practical Steps:
1. Right Now:
- Choose one thing to control
- Make one smart choice
- Plan one small victory
- Take action immediately
2. Today:
- Set reasonable limits
- Follow through
- Celebrate wins
- Stay strong
3. This Week:
- Build better habits
- Make wiser choices
- Control impulses
- Level up life

The Ultimate Self-Control Move:
Try to:
- Say no to instant gratification
- Choose what's right over what's easy
- Build better habits
- Be your own best friend (Warning: May result in actual maturity!)

Your Immediate Mission:
STOP READING AND:
1. Make one wise choice
2. Control one impulse

3. Choose long-term good
4. Start one good habit

Remember: Self-control isn't about being miserable - it's about being awesome!

Extra Credit: Try explaining to your friends why you're not joining the latest TikTok challenge. "I'm practicing self-control" sounds better than "My mom said no." 😊

P.S. - If controlling yourself was easy, everyone would be doing it. That's why you're going to be exceptional!

Final Tip: Think of self-control like being your own good parent - sometimes you have to tell yourself "no" for your own good!

Now go forth and master yourself! And remember: The hardest person to control is yourself, but it's also the most important! 💪

Chapter 33: How to Keep Your Heart On Track When It's Acting Like a GPS Having a Breakdown!

The "My Heart is All Over the Place" Challenge

Think having a focused heart means being a robot? Think emotions are your enemy? NOPE! Let's learn how to direct your heart without losing your personality!

What People THINK Heart Control Means:
- Never feeling anything
- Becoming emotionally constipated
- Turning into a walking statue
- Suppressing all feelings
- Living like a computer

What it ACTUALLY Means:
- Directing your feelings, not deleting them
- Keeping your heart GPS on track
- Having emotions without them having you
- Staying focused while staying human
- Being stable without being boring

The Daily Heart Direction Plan
Morning Heart Check:
1. The Quick Scan
- Is your heart chasing squirrels again?
- Are your feelings driving the bus?
- Where's your focus really at?
- What's distracting you today? (Note: Your crush doesn't count as a spiritual goal)
2. The Power Moves
- Point your heart toward good stuff
- Plan your focus points
- Set your emotional GPS (And no, not toward the ice cream shop)

Action Time! (Because Your Heart Won't Direct Itself)
Today's Missions:
☑ Direct your heart toward one good thing ☑ Catch one wandering emotion ☑ Focus on something that matters ☑ Choose your direction intentionally

Emergency Heart Protocols:
When your heart goes rogue:
1. Stop the emotional drift
2. Check your direction
3. Reset your focus
4. Get back on track (Note: It's okay if you have to do this 47 times today)

Your Weekly Focus Challenge:
Monday: "The Heart GPS"
- Set your daily direction
- Keep checking your course (Like a spiritual fitness tracker!)

Tuesday: "The Focus Finder"
- Catch wandering thoughts
- Direct them back to good (Yes, even during boring classes)

Wednesday: "The Direction Detector"
- Notice what grabs your heart

- Choose better attractions (Instagram influencers aren't life goals)

Practical Steps:
1. Right Now:
   - Check your heart's direction
   - Adjust your focus
   - Choose better targets
   - Take one step that way
2. Today:
   - Monitor your heart drift
   - Correct your course
   - Stay on target
   - Keep checking
3. This Week:
   - Build better focus habits
   - Choose better goals
   - Direct your attention
   - Stay consistent

The Ultimate Heart Direction Move:
Try to:
- Keep your heart on good things
- Direct your emotions wisely
- Focus on what matters
- Stay steady when distracted (Warning: May result in actual maturity!)

Your Immediate Mission:
STOP READING AND:
1. Check your heart's direction
2. Pick a better target
3. Take one step that way
4. Set up focus reminders

Remember: Your heart isn't bad, it just needs a better GPS signal!

Extra Credit: Try explaining why you're suddenly so focused. "I'm directing my heart" sounds better than "I'm trying not to think about pizza." 📡

P.S. - If keeping your heart focused was easy, everyone would be spiritual giants. That's why it's worth the effort!

Final Tip: Think of your heart like a puppy - it needs training, patience, and lots of redirection. But unlike a puppy, you can't blame your heart's mess on the carpet! 🐶

Now go forth and direct that heart! And remember: God gave you emotions for a reason, just make sure they're not the ones driving! 🚗

Chapter 34: How to Actually Love God When Netflix Exists!

The "Making God More Interesting Than Your Phone" Challenge

Think loving God means you can't have other interests? That spirituality and fun are enemies? NOPE! Let's learn how to make God your #1 while still living in the real world!

What People THINK Loving God Means:
- Deleting all your apps
- Never watching movies again
- Speaking in King James English
- Living in a church
- Becoming allergic to anything fun

What it ACTUALLY Means:
- Finding God in everything cool
- Making faith part of real life
- Having your best relationship ever
- Enjoying life God's way
- Living your best storyline

The Daily God-Love Plan

Morning Connection Check:
1. The Quick Reality Test
- What's getting more attention: God or TikTok?

- When's the last time you thought about God?
- Is your Bible app dustier than your games?
- Have you ghosted God lately? (Note: Liking Christian memes doesn't count as prayer)
2. The Power Moves
- Make God part of your fun
- Find Him in your favorites
- Include Him in everything (Yes, even while gaming - He's multitalented!)

Action Time! (Because Love Is a Verb, Not Just a Justin Bieber Song)
Today's Missions:
☑️ Find God in one fun thing ☑️ Make prayer actually interesting ☑️ Read Bible like it's Netflix ☑️ Have a real talk with God

Emergency Love Boosters:
When distractions hit:
1. Turn distraction into devotion
2. Make the boring beautiful
3. Find God in the fun
4. Make faith adventures (Note: Minecraft churches don't count as worship)

Your Weekly Love Challenge:
Monday: "The Fun Faith"
- Make prayer exciting
- Turn tasks into worship (Even homework can be holy... kind of)

Tuesday: "The God Hunt"
- Spot God in movies
- Find Him in music (Yes, even in non-Christian stuff!)

Wednesday: "The Joy Journey"
- Make faith fun
- Turn rules into relationships (It's about love, not laws!)

Practical Steps:
1. Right Now:
- Thank God for something fun
- Include Him in your plans

- Make one task worship
- Start an adventure with God
2. Today:
- Put God in your playlist
- Pray during games
- Find holy moments
- Make it real
3. This Week:
- Build better God-time
- Make faith personal
- Create cool traditions
- Keep it interesting

The Ultimate Love Move:
Try to:
- Make God your best friend
- Find Him everywhere
- Include Him in everything
- Keep it real and fun (Warning: May actually make faith awesome!)

Your Immediate Mission:
STOP READING AND:
1. Make one boring thing holy
2. Find God in something fun
3. Start a real conversation
4. Make faith an adventure

Remember: God invented fun - He's probably better at it than we are!

Extra Credit: Try explaining to your friends why you're smiling during math class. "I'm finding God in algebra" sounds better than "I'm losing my mind."

P.S. - If loving God is boring, you're probably doing it wrong. He created giraffes - clearly He has a sense of humor!

Final Tip: Think of God like the ultimate influencer - worth following, actually helpful, and won't try to sell you sketchy supplements!

Now go forth and make faith fun! And remember: You can love God AND have a life - He actually prefers it that way!

Chapter 35: How to Handle Temptation When Everything Looks Like a Cookie!

The "Not Every Shiny Thing is Good For You" Challenge

Think avoiding temptation means living in a bubble? Becoming immune to fun? NOPE! Let's learn how to dodge life's trap cards while still having a blast!

What People THINK Resisting Temptation Means:
- Never looking at anything fun
- Living in a cardboard box
- Wearing a blindfold forever
- Running away from everything
- Becoming a professional hermit

What it ACTUALLY Means:
- Being smart about choices
- Playing life on expert mode
- Leveling up your resistance stats
- Making better decisions
- Becoming actually strong

The Daily Temptation Defense Plan

Morning Setup:
1. The Quick Check
   - What's your weakness today?
   - Where are the danger zones?
   - Got your armor ready?
   - Emergency exits planned? (Note: "The devil made me do it" isn't a valid excuse)
2. The Power Moves
   - Plan your escape routes
   - Pack your resistance snacks
   - Set up your backup squad (Yes, having emergency chocolate is strategic)

Action Time! (Because Temptation Doesn't Take Naps)

Today's Missions:

☑☐ Spot one trap before it springs ☑☐ Choose good over tempting ☑☐ Help someone else resist ☑☐ Celebrate one victory

Emergency Resistance Protocols:
When temptation attacks:
1. RUN (literally if needed)
2. PHONE A FRIEND
3. EAT SOMETHING (hangry = vulnerable)
4. PRAY (God's always on call) (Note: All caps because this is IMPORTANT)

Your Weekly Defense Challenge:
Monday: "The Spot Check"
- Identify your kryptonite
- Plan your defenses (Knowing is half the battle!)

Tuesday: "The Strong Move"
- Resist one temptation
- Feel like a superhero (No cape required, but recommended)

Wednesday: "The Victory Dance"
- Celebrate good choices
- Build resistance muscles (Yes, victory dances count as exercise)

Practical Steps:
1. Right Now:
- Spot your weak points
- Make one good choice
- Plan your defenses
- Call your backup
2. Today:
- Avoid obvious traps
- Choose better options
- Stay strong in weak moments
- Keep snacks handy
3. This Week:
- Build resistance habits
- Create better choices
- Support others
- Track victories

The Ultimate Resistance Move:
Try to:

- Spot traps early
- Choose good consistently
- Help others resist
- Make it look easy (Warning: May result in actual character growth!)

Your Immediate Mission:
STOP READING AND:
1. Identify one weakness
2. Make one defense plan
3. Choose one good thing
4. Set up support system

Remember: Even Jesus was tempted - you're not weak for struggling, you're strong for resisting!

Extra Credit: Try explaining why you're running away from the donut table. "I'm practicing self-control" sounds better than "SUGAR IS MY WEAKNESS!" 😮

P.S. - If resisting temptation was easy, everyone would be saints. That's why it's impressive when you do it!

Final Tip: Think of temptation like pop-up ads in real life - annoying, persistent, but totally blockable with the right software! 💪

Now go forth and resist! And remember: Every temptation you beat is like leveling up in the game of life! 🎮

(Special Note: Keep emergency snacks in your locker. Sometimes the best way to fight temptation is with preparation... and protein bars! 🍫)

CopyRetry

L

rewrite NEXT CHAPTER. make sure it is funny and actionable
Edit

Chapter 36: How to Handle People's Drama Without Becoming Jerry Springer! 🎭

The "Not Getting Sucked into Everyone's Circus" Challenge

Think avoiding drama means becoming a monk? Living under a rock? NOPE! Let's learn how to stay above the chaos while keeping your sanity (and friends)!

What People THINK Drama-Free Means:

- Never talking to anyone
- Living in a pillow fort
- Becoming invisible
- Deleting all social media
- Moving to Antarctica

What it ACTUALLY Means:
- Being wise about people stuff
- Staying cool in chaos
- Making smart friend choices
- Keeping your peace
- Being drama-proof

The Daily Drama Defense Plan
Morning Setup:
1. The Quick Check
- Who's starting drama today?
- Where's the danger zone?
- Got your peace shield ready?
- Exit strategies planned? (Note: Hiding under your desk isn't a strategy)
2. The Power Moves
- Plan your peaceful responses
- Pack your chill pills
- Set up your quiet zones (Yes, bathroom breaks count as peace time)

Action Time! (Because Drama Never Takes a Vacation)
Today's Missions:
☑☐ Stay cool in one crazy situation ☑☐ Help calm someone else's drama ☑☐ Choose peace over gossip ☑☐ Be the eye of the storm

Emergency Peace Protocols:
When drama explodes:
1. Don't feed the chaos
2. Take deep breaths
3. Ask "Is this my circus?"
4. Choose peace (Note: Rolling your eyes doesn't count as peaceful)

Your Weekly Peace Challenge:

Monday: "The Drama Detector"
- Spot brewing storms
- Plan your calm (Being psychic about drama is a survival skill)

Tuesday: "The Peace Keeper"
- Stay cool when others don't
- Be the calm one (Sunglasses optional but recommended for extra cool points)

Wednesday: "The Wisdom Walker"
- Choose which fights aren't yours
- Master the art of "not my problem" (Professional level: Perfect the unbothered smile)

Practical Steps:
1. Right Now:
- Identify drama zones
- Plan peaceful responses
- Set up calm corners
- Practice your zen face
2. Today:
- Avoid drama magnets
- Choose peace actively
- Stay above chaos
- Keep your cool
3. This Week:
- Build peace habits
- Create drama-free zones
- Support other peace-seekers
- Perfect your exit strategies

Your Immediate Mission:
STOP READING AND:
1. Spot one drama source
2. Make one peace plan
3. Choose one calm response
4. Set up one quiet zone

Remember: Not every circus needs your acrobatic skills!
Extra Credit: Practice saying "That's interesting" when people bring drama. It's the Swiss Army knife of neutral responses! ☺

P.S. - If staying out of drama was easy, reality TV wouldn't exist. You're doing important work here!

Final Tip: Think of drama like a game of hot potato - you don't have to catch everything thrown at you! 🥔

Now go forth and keep your peace! And remember: Being drama-free doesn't mean being boring - it means being brilliantly unbothered! ✨

(Special Note: Keep headphones handy. Sometimes the best drama defense is pretending you can't hear it! 🎧)

Chapter 37: How to Give Up Your Ego Without Becoming a Doormat!

The "Getting Over Yourself Without Losing Yourself" Challenge
Think self-denial means becoming a human welcome mat? Saying yes to everything? NOPE! Let's learn how to surrender your ego while keeping your awesomeness!

What People THINK Self-Surrender Means:
- Never saying no to anyone
- Giving away all your stuff
- Living in a cardboard box
- Eating only plain oatmeal
- Becoming everyone's servant

What it ACTUALLY Means:
- Being free from your own drama
- Making room for better things
- Living without ego baggage
- Finding real freedom
- Becoming genuinely awesome

The Daily Ego Check Plan
Morning Setup:
1. The Quick Mirror Test
- Is your ego driving today?
- How many selfies planned?
- Need to always be right?

- Making everything about you? (Note: The world doesn't revolve around you... shocking, I know!)
2. The Power Moves
- Plan one selfless action
- Schedule some humility
- Arrange to help others (And no, posting about it doesn't count)

Action Time! (Because Your Ego Won't Deflate Itself)
Today's Missions:
☑☐ Do one thing without credit ☑☐ Let someone else shine
☑☐ Choose humility over pride ☑☐ Help without hashtags
Emergency Ego Control:
When pride attacks:
1. Remember you're not that special
2. Think of others first
3. Choose humility
4. Be genuinely helpful (Note: This might hurt at first)

Your Weekly Humility Challenge:
Monday: "The Invisible Helper"
- Do good secretly
- Don't post about it (The hardest part for most of us!)

Tuesday: "The Spotlight Shifter"
- Make others look good
- Share credit freely (Yes, even with your siblings)

Wednesday: "The Pride Buster"
- Admit when you're wrong
- Let others be right (Even when you're pretty sure you're right)

Practical Steps:
1. Right Now:
- Find one way to help secretly
- Let someone else win
- Share a victory
- Stay humble in success
2. Today:
- Do good anonymously
- Support others' success

- Choose team over self
- Keep quiet about wins
3. This Week:
- Build humility habits
- Create selfless patterns
- Support others quietly
- Perfect your invisible service

Your Immediate Mission:
STOP READING AND:
1. Do one secret good deed
2. Make someone else look good
3. Choose humility once
4. Help without recognition

Remember: True greatness doesn't need a spotlight!
Extra Credit: Try doing something awesome and NOT telling anyone. It's like being a superhero with a secret identity! 🦸‍♂️
P.S. - If giving up your ego was easy, social media wouldn't exist. You're doing holy work here!
Final Tip: Think of your ego like a balloon - sometimes it needs to be popped to keep you from floating away! 🎈
Now go forth and be humbly awesome! And remember: Real heroes don't need their name in lights - they're too busy helping others shine! ✨
(Special Note: Keep a secret good deed journal. It's like collecting achievement badges that only God can see! 📖)

Chapter 38: How to Let God Be Your Life's Project Manager (Without Micromanaging Him Back!)

The "Let God Run The Show" Challenge

Think letting God lead means becoming a spiritual robot? That divine guidance means losing all control? NOPE! Let's learn how to partner with the ultimate project manager!

What People THINK Divine Management Means:
- Never making any decisions
- Waiting for sky-writing from God
- Freezing until you hear angels sing
- Living in constant fear of choosing wrong
- Expecting burning bushes for breakfast choices

What it ACTUALLY Means:
- Having the ultimate life coach
- Getting divine strategy help
- Making better decisions
- Following the best game plan
- Having supernatural backup

The Daily Divine Partnership Plan
Morning Workflow:
1. The Quick Status Check
- Who's actually running your show?
- Are you backseat driving God again?
- Have you checked the master plan?
- Are you trying to hack God's timeline? (Note: God's WiFi doesn't need your hotspot)
2. The Power Moves
- Submit your daily agenda
- Check in with HQ (Heaven's Quarters)
- Align your goals with God's (Pro tip: His ideas are better than yours)

Action Time! (Because Faith Without Action is Just Wishful Thinking)
Today's Missions:
☑☐ Let God lead one decision ☑☐ Follow through on divine hints ☑☐ Trust the master plan ☑☐ Stop trying to control everything

Emergency Control-Freak Protocols:
When you're tempted to take over:
1. Remember who's really in charge

2. Take three chill pills
3. Trust the process
4. Let go of the steering wheel (Note: God doesn't need your backseat driving)

Your Weekly Surrender Challenge:

Monday: "The Trust Test"
- Let God handle one problem
- Don't try to fix everything (Yes, even that thing you're thinking about)

Tuesday: "The Flow Follower"
- Go with God's plan
- Stop fighting the current (Swimming upstream is exhausting anyway)

Wednesday: "The Peace Keeper"
- Accept divine timing
- Trust the process (Even when it seems slower than Internet Explorer)

Practical Steps:

1. Right Now:
- Hand over one worry
- Trust one outcome
- Follow one lead
- Let go of control

2. Today:
- Check in with God
- Follow His leads
- Trust His timing
- Stay in your lane

3. This Week:
- Build trust muscles
- Create divine habits
- Support God's plan
- Perfect your peace

Your Immediate Mission:

STOP READING AND:
1. Give God one problem
2. Trust one outcome

3. Follow one divine lead
4. Let go of something

Remember: God's got better plans than your best Pinterest board!

Extra Credit: Try explaining to friends why you're suddenly so chill. "God's got this" sounds better than "I'm having a nervous breakdown!" 😊

P.S. - If letting God lead was easy, we wouldn't all be control freaks. It's a process!

Final Tip: Think of God like the ultimate GPS - He knows the best route, even when you think you know a shortcut! 🗺️

Now go forth and let God lead! And remember: You're not losing control, you're upgrading to divine management! 🚀

(Special Note: Keep emergency chocolate handy for when trusting God gets hard. Sometimes spiritual growth needs sugar support! 🍫)

Chapter 39: How to Stay Focused When Your Brain Has 47 Browser Tabs Open!

The "Stop Getting Lost in Life's Distractions" Challenge

Think focusing on important stuff means becoming a boring productivity robot? That getting things done means no fun? NOPE! Let's learn how to actually focus without losing your personality!

What People THINK Focus Means:
- Living in a white room with no windows
- Deleting all fun apps forever
- Never watching another cat video
- Becoming allergic to social media
- Turning into a homework-only zombie

What it ACTUALLY Means:
- Getting important stuff done first
- Making room for both work and fun
- Being productive without being boring

- Finishing what matters
- Having time for what you love

The Daily Focus Plan
Morning Brain Setup:
1. The Quick Focus Check
- How many tabs open in your brain?
- Is TikTok living rent-free in your head?
- Can you remember what matters?
- Are you actually getting anything done? (Note: Scrolling isn't a productive activity)
2. The Power Moves
- Pick THREE important things
- Schedule focus blocks
- Plan your victories (Yes, breaks are allowed - they're actually important!)

Action Time! (Because Thinking About Doing Isn't Doing)
Today's Missions:
☑☐ Complete one important task ☑☐ Have focused time blocks ☑☐ Reduce distractions actively ☑☐ Finish something that matters

Emergency Focus Protocols:
When distraction attacks:
1. Close unnecessary brain tabs
2. Set a timer (25 minutes is magic)
3. Do ONE thing at a time
4. Reward real progress (Note: Checking Instagram isn't a reward)

Your Weekly Focus Challenge:
Monday: "The Task Tamer"
- Pick your top 3 priorities
- Actually do them first (Before checking any social media!)

Tuesday: "The Distraction Destroyer"
- Create focus zones
- Defend your time (Your phone doesn't control you!)

Wednesday: "The Completion Champion"
- Finish what you start

- Celebrate real wins (Getting things done feels better than scrolling)

Practical Steps:
1. Right Now:
   - Pick ONE important thing
   - Set a timer
   - Remove distractions
   - Just start
2. Today:
   - Use focus blocks
   - Take smart breaks
   - Track progress
   - Celebrate wins
3. This Week:
   - Build focus habits
   - Create work zones
   - Support progress
   - See real results

Your Immediate Mission:
STOP READING AND:
1. Choose one important task
2. Set a 25-minute timer
3. Remove all distractions
4. Actually start working

Remember: Focus isn't about perfection; it's about progress!
Extra Credit: Try explaining to friends why you're not responding instantly to texts. "I'm in my focus zone" sounds better than "I'm ignoring you!" 📱
P.S. - If staying focused was easy, nobody would ever finish reading a book!
Final Tip: Think of your brain like a smartphone - sometimes you need to close apps to run smoothly! 📱
Now go forth and focus! And remember: You can still have fun AFTER you get important stuff done! 🎮
(Special Note: Keep healthy snacks nearby - a hungry brain is a distracted brain! And no, scrolling through food pics doesn't count as eating! 🍎)

Bonus Tip: Name your distractions. It's harder to fall for "Fred the Facebook Temptation" when you call it out! 😄

Chapter 40: How to Stop Being Your Own Worst Critic (Without Becoming Your Biggest Fan!)

The "You're Not As Bad As You Think" Challenge
Think self-awareness means constant self-roasting? That humility means hating on yourself? NOPE! Let's learn how to be real without being really mean to yourself!

What People THINK Self-Assessment Means:
- Writing a list of all your fails
- Becoming your own personal bully
- Remembering every embarrassing moment
- Never celebrating victories
- Turning into a walking apology

What it ACTUALLY Means:
- Being honestly awesome AND humble
- Knowing your real strengths
- Admitting actual weaknesses
- Growing without groaning
- Improving without imploding

The Daily Reality Check Plan
Morning Mirror Talk:
1. The Quick Self-Check
   - Are you being too hard on yourself?
   - Did you forget your good points?
   - Are you comparing yourself to others?
   - Have you ghosted your own victories? (Note: That one fail doesn't define you)
2. The Power Moves
   - Find three good things about yourself
   - Admit one real area for growth
   - Plan one improvement (Without the drama, please!)

Action Time! (Because Self-Hate Isn't a Growth Strategy)
Today's Missions:
☑☐ Catch one negative self-thought ☑☐ Celebrate one real win
☑☐ Improve one actual thing ☑☐ Be kind to yourself once
Emergency Self-Talk Protocols:
When the inner critic attacks:
   1. Ask "Would I say this to a friend?"
   2. Find the actual truth
   3. Be realistically positive
   4. Make a fair assessment (Note: You wouldn't roast your bestie like this!)

Your Weekly Balance Challenge:
Monday: "The Truth Teller"
- List real strengths AND weaknesses
- No exaggeration either way (You're not perfect OR terrible)

Tuesday: "The Growth Gamer"
- Pick one thing to improve
- Actually work on it (Without the self-destructive commentary)

Wednesday: "The Victory Collector"
- Notice your wins
- Own your progress (Even small wins count!)

Practical Steps:
1. Right Now:
- Find one good thing about yourself
- Identify one real growth area
- Make one improvement plan
- Be honestly kind to yourself
2. Today:
- Catch negative self-talk
- Replace with truth
- Work on real growth
- Celebrate actual wins
3. This Week:
- Build balanced self-view
- Create growth habits

- Support your progress
- Keep it real

Your Immediate Mission:
STOP READING AND:
1. Write down three actual strengths
2. Pick one real area for growth
3. Make one improvement plan
4. Give yourself one honest compliment

Remember: You're neither the worst NOR the best - you're human!

Extra Credit: Try giving yourself a pep talk in the mirror without cringing. If you can't do it with a straight face, you're probably still too hard on yourself! 😊

P.S. - If being fair to yourself was easy, therapists wouldn't have jobs!

Final Tip: Think of yourself like a video game character - you've got strengths AND areas to level up! 🎮

Now go forth and be realistically awesome! And remember: God doesn't make junk, so stop treating yourself like you're broken! ✨

(Special Note: Keep a "Good Things About Me" list on your phone. When your inner critic starts ranting, pull it out and remind yourself that you're actually pretty cool! 📱)

Bonus Challenge: Try being as nice to yourself as you are to your pet. They're not perfect either, but you still think they're amazing! 🐶

Chapter 41: How to Not Care About Fame When Everyone's Chasing Clout!

The "Famous Doesn't Mean Fulfilled" Challenge

Think being unknown means being unsuccessful? That worth comes from follower count? NOPE! Let's learn how to be awesome without needing everyone to know it!

What People THINK Success Looks Like:
- Going viral on TikTok
- Having more followers than your school
- Getting verified on Instagram
- Becoming a meme
- Having your face everywhere

What REAL Success Actually Is:
- Being genuinely good
- Making actual impact
- Having real relationships
- Growing authentically
- Living purposefully

The Daily Reality Check Plan

Morning Fame Check:
1. The Quick Status Check
   - Are you living for likes?
   - Is your worth tied to views?
   - Do you need constant validation?
   - Are you performing or living? (Note: Your value isn't in your view count)
2. The Power Moves
   - Do one good thing secretly
   - Help someone without posting
   - Make impact without attention (Shocking concept: Good deeds without hashtags!)

Action Time! (Because Life Isn't a Reality Show)

Today's Missions:

☑☐ Do something without documenting it ☑☐ Be awesome in secret ☑☐ Value real relationships ☑☐ Make quiet impact

Emergency Fame-Craving Protocols:

When clout-chasing tempts you:
1. Remember what actually matters
2. Do something anonymous
3. Help without credit
4. Be quietly awesome (Note: The best things often happen off-camera)

Your Weekly Reality Challenge:

Monday: "The Secret Hero"
- Do good deeds anonymously
- Don't tell anyone (Yes, this means NO posting about it!)

Tuesday: "The Real Deal"
- Build actual relationships
- Have face-to-face conversations (Without checking your phone every 2 minutes)

Wednesday: "The Impact Maker"
- Create lasting value
- Focus on real results (Likes don't change the world)

Practical Steps:
1. Right Now:
   - Do one good thing secretly
   - Value one real relationship
   - Make one quiet impact
   - Be genuinely helpful
2. Today:
   - Live without documenting
   - Build authentic connections
   - Focus on actual value
   - Stay humble
3. This Week:
   - Create lasting impact
   - Develop real skills
   - Help anonymously
   - Make true friends

Your Immediate Mission:

STOP READING AND:
1. Delete one brag post
2. Do one anonymous good deed

3. Call (don't text!) a friend
4. Make real impact

Remember: Real legends don't need trending status!

Extra Credit: Try doing something awesome and NOT telling anyone. It's like being a superhero with a secret identity! ☐♂☐

P.S. - If your good deed doesn't have proof on social media, it still happened! (Mind-blowing, right?)

Final Tip: Think of life like an iceberg - the most important parts are usually the ones nobody sees! ☐

Now go forth and be quietly awesome! And remember: God doesn't have a social media account, and He's doing just fine! ✨

(Special Note: Start a secret good deed diary. It's like having a highlight reel that only you and God get to see! 📖)

Bonus Challenge: Try going a whole day without posting anything. The world won't end, promise! 😊 (But your battery life will thank you!)

Chapter 42: How to Not Base Your Happiness on Other People's Moods!

The "Your Peace Isn't Their Property" Challenge

Think you need everyone's approval to be happy? That your mood depends on their faces? NOPE! Let's learn how to keep your joy even when others are being joy-vampires!

What People THINK Peace Depends On:
- Everyone liking you
- No one being mad at you
- Getting constant validation
- Perfect relationships
- Zero drama ever

What REAL Peace Actually Is:
- Being stable despite drama
- Keeping cool when others can't
- Having joy regardless of others
- Standing firm in chaos

133

- Being unshakeable inside

The Daily Independence Plan
Morning Peace Check:
1. The Quick Status Check
- Is your mood on someone else's leash?
- Are you emotional Velcro?
- Does others' drama become yours?
- Are you a feelings sponge? (Note: You're not responsible for everyone's happiness)
2. The Power Moves
- Set your own emotional thermostat
- Choose your mood intentionally
- Build your peace fortress (Your joy doesn't need their permission!)

Action Time! (Because Peace Is An Inside Job)
Today's Missions:
☑☐ Keep your cool when others don't ☑☐ Stay happy despite complaints ☑☐ Choose peace in chaos ☑☐ Be stable when everything isn't

Emergency Drama Defense Protocols:
When others try to shake your peace:
1. Remember it's their stuff, not yours
2. Keep your emotional boundaries
3. Choose your own mood
4. Stay in your peace zone (Note: Their circus isn't your circus)

Your Weekly Independence Challenge:
Monday: "The Mood Master"
- Set your own emotional tone
- Keep it despite others (Yes, even when they're super grumpy)

Tuesday: "The Peace Keeper"
- Maintain your calm in chaos
- Don't catch their stress (You're not a feelings vacuum cleaner)

Wednesday: "The Joy Guardian"
- Protect your happiness

- Share without absorbing (Be a lighthouse, not a sponge)

Practical Steps:
1. Right Now:
- Choose your mood
- Set emotional boundaries
- Protect your peace
- Stay stable
2. Today:
- Keep your joy
- Resist mood vampires
- Stay centered
- Be unshakeable
3. This Week:
- Build peace habits
- Create joy barriers
- Support without absorbing
- Master your mood

Your Immediate Mission:
STOP READING AND:
1. Choose your mood
2. Set one boundary
3. Protect your peace
4. Stay stable in chaos

Remember: Your joy doesn't need their approval!
Extra Credit: Try staying happy when someone's complaining. You're not being mean; you're being mentally healthy! ☺
P.S. - Other people's moods are like weather - you can't control them, but you can bring an umbrella!
Final Tip: Think of your peace like your phone password - not everyone gets access! 🔒
Now go forth and keep your joy! And remember: You can care about people without carrying their emotions! ✨
(Special Note: Create a peace playlist for when others try to shake your mood. Sometimes you need backup music for your emotional boundaries! ♪)
Bonus Challenge: Try having a good day even when others are having a bad one. It's not selfish - it's sanity! ✹

135

Chapter 43: How to Not Be a Know-It-All While Actually Knowing Stuff!

The "Smart Without Being Annoying" Challenge
Think being knowledgeable means correcting everyone? That wisdom means being Wikipedia with legs? NOPE! Let's learn how to be smart without making everyone roll their eyes!

What People THINK Knowledge Means:
- Starting every sentence with "Actually..."
- Correcting people's grammar
- Showing off random facts
- Being a walking Google
- Making others feel dumb

What REAL Wisdom Is:
- Knowing when to share
- Using knowledge to help
- Learning from everyone
- Staying humble while smart
- Making others feel valued

The Daily Wisdom Check

Morning Brain Check:
1. The Quick Smart Scan
   - Are you being a know-it-all?
   - Do you interrupt to correct?
   - Is your knowledge helping?
   - Are you listening or just waiting to talk? (Note: Not everything needs your expert opinion)
2. The Power Moves
   - Share only when asked
   - Help without showing off
   - Learn while teaching (Your brain isn't a weapon, it's a tool!)

Action Time! (Because Smart Is How You Share, Not What You Know)

Today's Missions:
☑☐ Listen more than you speak ☑☐ Help without humiliating
☑☐ Learn something new ☑☐ Share wisely when asked

Emergency Know-It-All Protocols:
When tempted to show off:
1. Bite your tongue
2. Ask questions instead
3. Listen to learn
4. Share only if helpful (Note: Sometimes the smartest thing is silence)

Your Weekly Wisdom Challenge:
Monday: "The Humble Scholar"
- Learn from someone younger
- Ask questions you "should" know (Your ego can handle it)

Tuesday: "The Helpful Expert"
- Share knowledge only when useful
- Make others feel smart (No "well, actually" allowed)

Wednesday: "The Wisdom Seeker"
- Learn something new
- Admit what you don't know (It's actually impressive!)

Practical Steps:
1. Right Now:
- Hold one correction
- Ask one genuine question
- Learn from someone else
- Share only if asked
2. Today:
- Listen more than talk
- Help without showing off
- Stay humble about knowledge
- Make others feel valued
3. This Week:
- Build learning habits
- Create helping patterns
- Support others' growth
- Perfect your humility

Your Immediate Mission:
STOP READING AND:
1. Resist one correction
2. Learn from someone unexpected
3. Share only when asked
4. Make someone feel smart

Remember: True wisdom makes others feel capable, not stupid!
Extra Credit: Try getting through a whole conversation without correcting anyone. Yes, even when they say "literally" wrong! ☺
P.S. - Being the smartest person in the room isn't as cool as making the room smarter together!
Final Tip: Think of knowledge like seasoning - a little at the right time is perfect; too much ruins everything! 🧂
Now go forth and be wisely humble! And remember: Even Einstein didn't go around correcting everyone's math! ✨
(Special Note: Keep a "Things I Don't Know" journal. It's humbling, and it gives you new things to learn! 📚)
Bonus Challenge: Let someone explain something you already know. Their perspective might teach you something new! 🎓

Chapter 44: How to Not Stress About Everything When The World's Gone Crazy!

The "Stay Chill When Everything's Wild" Challenge
Think managing external chaos means becoming a hermit? That peace means controlling everything? NOPE! Let's learn how to stay cool when the world's doing its thing!

What People THINK Peace Means:
- Controlling every situation
- Fixing everyone's problems
- Worrying about all news
- Managing everything
- Never letting life happen

What REAL Peace Actually Is:
- Letting stuff be stuff

138

- Managing what's yours
- Ignoring what isn't
- Staying zen in chaos
- Choosing your battles

The Daily Chaos Management Plan
Morning Reality Check:
1. The Quick Stress Scan
- Are you carrying the world?
- Is it actually your problem?
- Can you even control this?
- Should you care about this? (Note: Not your circus, not your monkeys!)
2. The Power Moves
- Focus on your lane
- Let others handle theirs
- Control the controllable (Revolutionary idea: Some stuff isn't your business!)

Action Time! (Because Stress Isn't a Hobby)
Today's Missions:
☑☐ Mind your own business once ☑☐ Let something be messy
☑☐ Don't fix someone's problem ☑☐ Stay in your lane

Emergency Stress Protocols:
When everything's crazy:
1. Ask "Is this mine to fix?"
2. Choose what matters
3. Let the rest be
4. Stay in your zone (Note: The world spun before you got here)

Your Weekly Peace Challenge:
Monday: "The Drama Dodger"
- Skip three problems that aren't yours
- Watch the world not end (Shocking: Things work out without you!)

Tuesday: "The Peace Keeper"
- Focus on your stuff
- Let others handle theirs (Their mess isn't your assignment)

Wednesday: "The Zen Master"
- Stay cool in chaos
- Let things be imperfect (Perfect is boring anyway)

Practical Steps:
1. Right Now:
- Drop one worry that's not yours
- Focus on your actual job
- Let something be messy
- Choose peace over control
2. Today:
- Mind your business
- Skip optional drama
- Stay in your lane
- Keep your peace
3. This Week:
- Build boundary habits
- Create peace zones
- Support without absorbing
- Master your chill

Your Immediate Mission:
STOP READING AND:
1. Drop one not-your-problem
2. Focus on your actual stuff
3. Let something be imperfect
4. Choose peace over control

Remember: Not everything needs your attention!

Extra Credit: Try watching someone solve their own problem without your help. They might surprise you! ☺

P.S. - The world managed before you showed up and will manage after your nap!

Final Tip: Think of life like a TV show - you can't control the plot, but you can choose your channel! 📺

Now go forth and keep your peace! And remember: Being chill isn't being careless - it's being smart! ✨

(Special Note: Create a "Not My Problem" list. It's surprisingly freeing to write down what you DON'T have to fix! 📝)

Bonus Challenge: Let something be messy for a whole day. The universe won't collapse, promise! ☐

Chapter 45: How to Not Believe Everything You Hear (Without Becoming a Total Skeptic)!

The "Don't Be Gullible But Don't Be Grumpy" Challenge
Think wisdom means either believing everything or trusting no one? NOPE! Let's learn how to be smart without turning into a conspiracy theorist!

What People THINK Discernment Means:
- Doubting literally everything
- Trusting absolutely nothing
- Wearing a tinfoil hat
- Seeing plots everywhere
- Never believing anyone

What REAL Wisdom Actually Is:
- Being smartly selective
- Thinking before believing
- Checking good sources
- Trusting wisely
- Balancing faith and facts

The Daily Truth Check Plan
Morning Reality Check:
1. The Quick Truth Scan
- Are you believing blindly?
- Are you doubting needlessly?
- Is this source trustworthy?
- Does this make actual sense? (Note: Not everything on TikTok is true!)
2. The Power Moves
- Check before sharing
- Think before believing

- Trust but verify (Revolutionary idea: Facts are still a thing!)

Action Time! (Because Wisdom Needs Action)
Today's Missions:
☑☐ Fact-check one thing ☑☐ Question one assumption ☑☐ Find reliable sources ☑☐ Share truth responsibly

Emergency Wisdom Protocols:
When facing questionable info:
1. Ask "Says who?"
2. Check reliable sources
3. Think it through
4. Wait before sharing (Note: Being first isn't as cool as being right)

Your Weekly Truth Challenge:
Monday: "The Fact Finder"
- Check before believing
- Research before sharing (Google is free, use it!)

Tuesday: "The Truth Seeker"
- Question kindly
- Verify wisely (Without becoming paranoid)

Wednesday: "The Wisdom Walker"
- Balance trust and doubt
- Share responsibility (Truth matters, spread it well)

Practical Steps:
1. Right Now:
- Check one "fact"
- Question one claim
- Find good sources
- Share truth carefully
2. Today:
- Think critically
- Research well
- Trust wisely
- Stay balanced
3. This Week:
- Build wisdom habits
- Create truth filters

- Support real facts
- Master discernment

Your Immediate Mission:
STOP READING AND:
1. Fact-check something
2. Find reliable sources
3. Question assumptions
4. Share truth responsibly

Remember: Not everything needs to be shared or believed!

Extra Credit: Try finding three sources before sharing that "mind-blowing fact" in the group chat! ☐

P.S. - Just because it has a lot of likes doesn't make it true!

Final Tip: Think of your mind like a doorman - not everyone gets in just because they showed up! 🚪

Now go forth and be wisely discerning! And remember: You can be smart without being cynical! ✨

(Special Note: Keep a "Verified Truth" journal. It's amazing how many "facts" don't make the cut! 📖)

Bonus Challenge: Wait 24 hours before sharing something shocking. Most fake news solves itself! ☐

Extra Wisdom Note:
- If it seems too good to be true... it probably is
- If it makes you super angry... check twice
- If your grandma would love sharing it... verify it
- If it confirms all your beliefs... question it harder

Because sometimes the smartest thing you can say is "Let me check on that!" ☐

Chapter 46: How to Handle Haters Without Becoming One!

The "Stay Golden When They Go Dark" Challenge
Think handling criticism means either crying or revenge? NOPE! Let's learn how to deal with hate while keeping your awesome intact!

What People THINK Handling Haters Means:
- Planning epic comebacks
- Writing angry journal entries
- Plotting revenge scenarios
- Becoming a supervillain
- Moving to Antarctica

What REAL Strength Actually Is:
- Staying cool under fire
- Growing from criticism
- Rising above drama
- Keeping your joy
- Learning while winning

The Daily Strength Plan
Morning Shield Check:
1. The Quick Defense Scan
- Is their opinion rent-free in your head?
- Are you letting haters win?
- Has criticism crushed your vibe?
- Are you still awesome? (Note: Their words don't define your worth!)
2. The Power Moves
- Choose joy anyway
- Use criticism to grow
- Stay awesome regardless (Revolutionary idea: Success is the best revenge!)

Action Time! (Because Winning Needs Action)
Today's Missions:
☑☐ Stay positive despite shade ☑☐ Learn from valid criticism
☑☐ Keep your cool under fire ☑☐ Be awesome anyway

Emergency Hater Protocols:

When the hate hits:
1. Take a deep breath
2. Find the lesson (if any)
3. Keep your class
4. Level up anyway (Note: Getting bitter never made anyone better)

Your Weekly Strength Challenge:
Monday: "The Joy Keeper"
- Stay happy despite hate
- Keep winning anyway (Success really is the best comeback)

Tuesday: "The Growth Gainer"
- Learn from valid points
- Ignore useless noise (Not all criticism is useful)

Wednesday: "The Peace Pro"
- Stay cool under fire
- Keep your awesome intact (Your joy is your superpower)

Practical Steps:
1. Right Now:
- Choose your response
- Pick what's useful
- Drop what's not
- Keep shining
2. Today:
- Stay positive
- Learn what helps
- Ignore what hurts
- Keep growing
3. This Week:
- Build resilience
- Create joy shields
- Support others
- Master peace

Your Immediate Mission:
STOP READING AND:
1. Find one useful lesson

2. Drop one useless comment
3. Choose joy anyway
4. Keep being awesome

Remember: Haters are just fans in denial!

Extra Credit: Turn their shade into your sunshine - use criticism as motivation to level up! ✦

P.S. - Sometimes people throw shade because they can't handle your light!

Final Tip: Think of haters like sandpaper - they might try to rough you up, but you end up polished! ✧

Now go forth and shine anyway! And remember: The best response to hate is becoming even more awesome! 🌀

(Special Note: Start a "Victory Journal" - write down your wins to read when haters try to bring you down! 📖)

Bonus Challenge: Help someone else dealing with haters. Your experience can be their strength! 💪

Extra Wisdom:
- If they criticize your path, walk it louder
- If they doubt your dreams, dream bigger
- If they question your worth, level up
- If they can't handle your shine, get brighter

Because sometimes the best way to handle haters is to be so busy being awesome you forget they exist! ✦

Remember: God didn't give you this light for you to dim it because others can't handle the brightness!

Chapter 47: How to Boss Life When Life is Being a Boss!

The "Everything's Hard But I'm Harder" Challenge
Think tough times mean game over? That challenges are the end? NOPE! Let's learn how to level up when life's trying to level you down!

What People THINK Handling Struggles Means:
- Crying in your cereal
- Becoming a professional complainer
- Writing sad Instagram captions
- Giving up completely
- Living under your blanket forever

What REAL Toughness Is:
- Growing through problems
- Getting stronger in storms
- Finding joy in chaos
- Learning while losing
- Winning eventually

The Daily Victory Plan
Morning Battle Check:
1. The Quick Strength Scan
- Are you letting problems win?
- Is difficulty defeating you?
- Have you forgotten your power?
- Are you still fighting? (Note: Tough times are temporary, but tough people last!)
2. The Power Moves
- Choose victory mindset
- Find strength in struggle
- Keep pushing forward (Mind-blowing idea: Problems are just strength training!)

Action Time! (Because Winners Keep Moving)
Today's Missions:
☑☐ Face one hard thing ☑☐ Find joy in struggle ☑☐ Learn from difficulty ☑☐ Keep going anyway

Emergency Strength Protocols:

When life hits hard:
1. Remember who you are
2. Find the growth opportunity
3. Keep your joy
4. Push through anyway (Note: The storm can't last forever)

Your Weekly Warrior Challenge:
Monday: "The Problem Crusher"
- Face difficulties head-on
- Find victory in valleys (Tough times = free strength training)

Tuesday: "The Joy Fighter"
- Choose happiness in hardship
- Keep smiling through storms (Your joy is your weapon)

Wednesday: "The Growth Gainer"
- Learn from every loss
- Get stronger through struggle (Problems are just practice)

Practical Steps:
1. Right Now:
- Face one challenge
- Find one lesson
- Choose one victory
- Keep moving forward
2. Today:
- Handle what's hard
- Learn what helps
- Stay in the fight
- Keep growing
3. This Week:
- Build resilience
- Create victory habits
- Support others
- Master challenges

Your Immediate Mission:
STOP READING AND:
1. Face something tough

2. Find one good thing
3. Make one step forward
4. Keep fighting strong

Remember: Tough times don't last, tough people do!

Extra Credit: Help someone else who's struggling - your battle scars might be their battle map! 💪

P.S. - Sometimes God lets you go through stuff so you can help others through similar stuff!

Final Tip: Think of problems like video game levels - each one makes you stronger for the next! 🎮

Now go forth and conquer! And remember: You're the hero of your story, not the victim! ❌

(Special Note: Create a "Victory Map" - mark every win, no matter how small. They add up to big victories! 🗺️)

Bonus Challenge: Turn your biggest problem into your biggest testimony!

Extra Warrior Wisdom:
- If the problem looks big, you look bigger
- If the storm seems strong, you be stronger
- If the path seems hard, you get harder
- If life pushes you, push back harder

Because sometimes the toughest times are just prep for your greatest victories! 🏆

Remember: God doesn't give you battles He hasn't already prepared you to win! Trust the process and keep fighting! 🙏

Chapter 48: How to Think About Eternity Without Having an Existential Crisis!

The "Forever Is a Long Time But Don't Panic" Challenge

Think contemplating eternity means becoming a cave-dwelling philosopher? NOPE! Let's learn how to handle the big picture while still enjoying the small stuff!

What People THINK Eternal Perspective Means:
- Never enjoying anything temporal
- Becoming allergic to fun
- Staring into space constantly
- Writing deep poems about existence
- Giving away your PlayStation

What REAL Eternal Perspective Is:
- Making choices that matter forever
- Building lasting impact
- Enjoying life with wisdom
- Investing in what counts
- Living with purpose

The Daily Eternity Check

Morning Reality Check:
1. The Quick Forever Scan
    - Are your choices eternal-friendly?
    - Is this gonna matter in heaven?
    - Are you building something lasting?
    - Are you balancing now and forever? (Note: You can enjoy pizza AND plan for eternity!)
2. The Power Moves
    - Make eternal investments
    - Build lasting relationships
    - Create meaningful impact (Revolutionary idea: You can have fun AND be deep!)

Action Time! (Because Forever Starts Now)

Today's Missions:

☑☐ Do one thing that lasts ☑☐ Build one real relationship ☑☐ Make eternal impact ☑☐ Enjoy life wisely

Emergency Eternity Protocols:

When existential crisis hits:
1. Remember God's got this
2. Focus on what matters
3. Take eternal action
4. Stay present and purposeful (Note: Don't forget to breathe - you still need oxygen!)

Your Weekly Eternal Challenge:
Monday: "The Forever Builder"
- Make lasting choices
- Build eternal value (While still enjoying your tacos)

Tuesday: "The Impact Maker"
- Create meaningful moments
- Invest in forever stuff (Yes, video games can wait)

Wednesday: "The Balance Master"
- Mix eternal and temporal
- Live now with forever in mind (It's possible to do both!)

Practical Steps:
1. Right Now:
- Choose one eternal investment
- Build one lasting thing
- Make one wise choice
- Live purposefully
2. Today:
- Balance fun and forever
- Create lasting impact
- Enjoy life wisely
- Build what matters
3. This Week:
- Develop eternal perspective
- Create lasting habits
- Support eternal values
- Master the balance

Your Immediate Mission:
STOP READING AND:
1. Do something lasting
2. Build real relationships
3. Make wise choices

4. Enjoy life eternally

Remember: You're not just living for the weekend!

Extra Credit: Explain eternity to your pet - their confused face will help you keep perspective! 🐶

P.S. - Living for eternity doesn't mean you can't enjoy Netflix. Just don't let Netflix be your life's purpose!

Final Tip: Think of life like a game save file - what you do now affects your eternal playthrough! 🎮

Now go forth and live eternally! And remember: You can think deep thoughts AND enjoy memes! ✨

(Special Note: Keep an "Eternal Impact" journal - track choices that'll matter forever! 📖)

Bonus Challenge: Do something today that'll matter in 1000 years! (Hint: It probably involves helping people)

Extra Eternal Wisdom:
- If it won't matter in eternity, don't stress about it
- If it will matter forever, invest more in it
- If it's temporary, enjoy it without idolizing it
- If it's eternal, prioritize it

Because sometimes the most eternal thing you can do is love someone well right now! ❤️

Remember: God invented both eternity AND ice cream - you can appreciate both! 🍦

Chapter 49: How to Be Hyped for Heaven Without Checking Out Early!

The "Living for Forever Without Missing Today" Challenge

Think eternal life is just sitting on clouds playing harps? NOPE! Let's get excited about the ultimate endgame while still crushing it in the current levels!

What People THINK Desiring Heaven Means:
- Becoming useless on Earth
- Never enjoying current life
- Walking around in a daze
- Constantly muttering prayers
- Being "too heavenly minded for earthly good"

What REAL Eternal Desire Is:
- Training for the ultimate upgrade
- Building your eternal high score
- Prepping for the final boss battle
- Making choices that last
- Living like you've read the spoilers

The Daily Forever Prep

Morning Eternity Check:
1. The Quick Heaven Scan
- Are you prepping for promotion?
- Building eternal achievements?
- Collecting divine XP?
- Making forever-relevant choices? (Note: Earth is your training ground, not your waiting room!)
2. The Power Moves
- Live like tomorrow's launch day
- Train for eternal upgrades
- Stack up heavenly achievements (Pro tip: Kindness gives major eternal XP!)

Action Time! (Because Heaven's Not for Spectators)

Today's Missions:

☑☐ Do one eternally relevant thing ☑☐ Help someone toward heaven ☑☐ Make choices future-you will thank you for ☑☐ Stack up divine achievements

Emergency Perspective Reset:
When Earth gets too heavy:
1. Remember the endgame
2. Focus on eternal rewards
3. Think ultimate upgrade
4. Keep eternal momentum (Note: Don't rage quit - the rewards are worth it!)

Your Weekly Eternal Challenge:
Monday: "The Forever Builder"
- Make choices future-you will high-five you for
- Stack up heavenly achievements (Yes, being nice to your siblings counts!)

Tuesday: "The Eternal Investor"
- Put time in things that last
- Build divine portfolio (Spoiler: Love has the best returns)

Practical Steps:
1. Right Now:
- Choose one eternal investment
- Help someone heavenward
- Make one forever-choice
- Think ultimate rewards
2. Today:
- Live like it matters forever
- Train for eternal purposes
- Build lasting impact
- Keep heaven in mind

Your Immediate Mission:
STOP READING AND:
1. Do something heaven-worthy
2. Help someone on their journey
3. Make one eternal investment
4. Live like you know the ending

Remember: You're training for eternity, not just existing!

Extra Credit: Explain heaven to your goldfish - their attention span might match most people's eternal perspective! 🙂

P.S. - Heaven is like the ultimate DLC, but you gotta play the main game well first!
Final Tip: Think of Earth like the tutorial level - every challenge is prep for the real game! 🎮
Now go forth and level up eternally! And remember: Being heavenly-minded can make you incredibly earthly-useful! ✦
Bonus Challenge: Do something today that angels would leave 5-star reviews for!
Key Strategy Points:
- Good deeds = Eternal achievements
- Kindness = Divine XP
- Love = Highest scoring moves
- Helping others = Multiplayer bonus points

Because sometimes the best way to desire heaven is to bring a bit of it to Earth! ✦
Remember: God's got the cheat codes to life, and He's sharing them in His guidebook! 📖

Chapter 50: How to Hand Your Mess to God Without Dropping Your Pizza!

The "Everything's Chaos But I'm Trusting God" Challenge

Think surrendering to God means having your life perfectly together? That you need color-coded prayer journals and matching Bible highlighters? NOPE! Let's learn how to trust God even when your life looks like a teenager's room!

What Messy Surrender Isn't:
- Having perfect prayer posture
- Speaking in King James English
- Pretending you've got it together
- Being a spiritual Instagram influencer
- Hiding your chaos under holy hashtags

What Real Surrender Is:
- Bringing God your actual mess
- Trusting Him with your chaos
- Being real about your struggles
- Letting Him handle your drama
- Accepting divine help while being human

The Daily Mess Management Plan

Morning Reality Check:
1. The Quick Chaos Scan
   - Is your life a beautiful disaster?
   - Are you pretending you're fine?
   - Need some divine intervention?
   - Ready to let God take the wheel? (Note: He's seen worse, trust me!)
2. The Honest Moves
   - Admit what's actually wrong
   - Hand over real problems
   - Accept heavenly help (Revolutionary idea: God loves messy people!)

Action Time! (Because Faith Without Action is Just Wishful Thinking)

Today's Real Missions:

☑☐ Be honest about one struggle ☑☐ Give God one actual problem ☑☐ Trust Him with something specific ☑☐ Accept help without fake perfection

Emergency God Handoff Protocol:
When life's totally sideways:
1. Stop trying to fix everything
2. Hand it to God (yes, ALL of it)
3. Let Him actually help
4. Follow His lead (Note: No need to prettify your problems - He sees them anyway!)

Your Weekly Surrender Challenge:
Monday: "The Real Deal"
- Tell God exactly how it is
- No spiritual filter needed (He already knows, but He loves when you're honest)

Tuesday: "The Divine Handoff"
- Give Him your biggest mess
- Let Him actually handle it (Watching Him work is better than Netflix)

Practical Steps:
1. Right Now:
- Identify your biggest chaos
- Hand it over honestly
- Trust His process
- Follow His lead
2. Today:
- Keep it real with God
- Let Him work
- Trust His timing
- Stay in His lane

Your Immediate Mission:
STOP READING AND:
1. Name your actual mess
2. Give it to God (for real)
3. Trust His process
4. Watch Him work

Remember: God's specialty is fixing messes - that's why He made teenagers!

Extra Credit: Try explaining your problems to God like you'd tell your best friend - He can handle your real talk!

P.S. - The difference between a mess and a message is usually just God's intervention!

Now go forth and trust! And remember: God doesn't need you to clean up before coming to Him - He's more like a divine emergency room than a fancy spa! ✝

(Special Note: Sometimes the most spiritual thing you can do is admit you're not feeling spiritual at all!)

Bonus Challenge: Give God something you've been pretending you can handle. Spoiler alert: He already knows you can't! ☺

Because sometimes surrender looks less like a beautiful spiritual Instagram post and more like collapsing on your bed saying "God, HELP!"

Chapter 51: How to Do Small Things Without Feeling Like a Small Fry!

The "Size Doesn't Matter" Challenge

Think you need to change the world before breakfast? That only huge achievements count? NOPE! Let's learn how to make small moves with massive impact!

What People Think Matters:
- Going viral on social media
- Starting a global movement
- Becoming an overnight success
- Creating world peace before lunch
- Having a TED talk by age 15

What Actually Counts:
- Being kind when no one's watching
- Helping one person at a time
- Making tiny consistent moves
- Doing small things with love
- Building block by block

The Daily Small Wins Plan

Morning Reality Check:
1. The Quick Size Scan
- Are you overlooking small wins?
- Waiting for massive moments?
- Missing tiny opportunities?
- Ignoring daily chances? (Note: Mother Teresa started by helping ONE person!)
2. The Mini Power Moves
- Find tiny ways to help
- Make small improvements
- Create little impacts (Plot twist: Small actions = Big results!)

Action Time! (Because Every Drop Makes an Ocean)

Today's Bite-Size Missions:

☑☐ Do one tiny good deed ☑☐ Improve one small thing ☑☐ Help in a little way ☑☐ Make a mini difference

Emergency Perspective Protocol:

When feeling insignificant:
1. Start super small
2. Focus on one thing
3. Make it count
4. Keep building (Note: Rome wasn't built in a TikTok!)

Your Weekly Mini Challenge:
Monday: "The Little Legend"
- Rock the small stuff
- Own the tiny wins (Picking up trash counts as world-changing!)

Tuesday: "The Micro Master"
- Perfect tiny actions
- Celebrate small victories (Making your bed is basically saving the world)

Practical Steps:
1. Right Now:
- Find one small opportunity
- Take one tiny action
- Make one mini impact
- Start somewhere small
2. Today:
- Look for little chances
- Create small wins
- Build tiny habits
- Make mini progress

Your Immediate Mission:
STOP READING AND:
1. Do one small good thing
2. Fix one tiny problem
3. Help in a minor way
4. Create a mini victory

Remember: Mustard seeds change landscapes!
Extra Credit: Make your bed like you're changing the universe - because small habits lead to big changes! □□
P.S. - Jesus started with 12 guys, and look how that turned out! Now go forth and rock the small stuff! And remember: Every massive success started with someone doing something tiny! ★

Bonus Challenge: Find the smallest possible way to help someone today. Then watch how it grows!
Key Truth Bombs:
- Small actions > Big plans
- Tiny steps > Giant leaps
- Little kindness > Huge ambitions
- Mini consistency > Massive one-offs

Because sometimes the biggest impacts start with the smallest actions! And hey, even superheroes have to put their pants on one leg at a time! 🦸

Remember: God specializes in using small things to make big changes. Just ask David about his little rock collection! □

Chapter 52: How to Stay Humble Without Becoming a Human Doormat!

The "Humble but Not Hopeless" Challenge
Think being humble means constantly roasting yourself? That you need to pretend you're terrible at everything? NOPE! Let's learn how to keep it real without losing your sparkle!

What People Think Humility Is:
- Never accepting compliments
- Pretending you're bad at stuff
- Adding "just" to everything you do
- Being everyone's personal carpet
- Apologizing for breathing

What Real Humility Is:
- Knowing your worth without the ego
- Accepting praise with grace
- Owning your gifts while staying grounded
- Being confident AND kind
- Keeping it real all around

The Daily Humble Check
Morning Balance Scan:
1. The Quick Reality Check

- Are you fake-humble-bragging?
- Playing smaller than you are?
- Hiding your actual talents?
- Being honest about yourself? (Note: False modesty is just pride in a cheap disguise!)

2. The Balanced Moves
- Own your skills honestly
- Accept praise gracefully
- Help others shine too (Mind-blow: You can be awesome AND humble!)

Action Time! (Because Humility is a Verb)
Today's Real Missions:
☑☐ Accept one compliment properly ☑☐ Share credit genuinely ☑☐ Own one talent honestly ☑☐ Help someone else shine

Emergency Balance Protocol:
When pride or self-deprecation attacks:
1. Get real with yourself
2. Find the middle ground
3. Stay authentically humble
4. Keep your worth intact (Note: You can be a diamond AND be down-to-earth!)

Your Weekly Balance Challenge:
Monday: "The Real Deal"
- Be honest about your skills
- Share the spotlight willingly (No need to dim your light to let others shine)

Tuesday: "The Grace Ace"
- Accept praise properly
- Give credit freely (It's okay to be good at stuff!)

Practical Steps:
1. Right Now:
- Own one real talent
- Share one genuine compliment
- Accept praise gracefully
- Stay grounded but great
2. Today:

- Be honestly awesome
- Help others up
- Stay authentically humble
- Keep it balanced

Your Immediate Mission:
STOP READING AND:
1. Accept a compliment properly
2. Own one real talent
3. Help someone else shine
4. Stay genuinely humble

Remember: Even Jesus didn't pretend He couldn't do miracles!

Extra Credit: Try saying "Thank you" instead of "Oh, it was nothing" when someone compliments you. Revolutionary, right? ☺

P.S. - Moses was called the most humble man on earth, and he still led a nation!

Now go forth and be humbly awesome! And remember: Being humble doesn't mean thinking less of yourself, it means thinking of yourself less! ★

Bonus Challenge: List three things you're actually good at without adding "but" or "just" to the end!

Key Truth Bombs:
- Real humility has good posture
- True modesty knows its worth
- Authentic humility helps others rise
- Genuine humbleness spreads light

Because sometimes the most humble thing you can do is honestly own who God made you to be! ✦

Remember: You can be a masterpiece AND a work in progress at the same time! Both/and, not either/or! 🎨

Chapter 53: How to Stay Spiritual When Everything's Screaming "MATERIAL GIRL!"

The "Spirit Over Stuff" Challenge

Think being spiritual means trading your iPhone for a stone tablet? That you need to become allergic to nice things? NOPE! Let's learn how to keep your soul lit while living in the real world!

What People Think Spiritual Living Means:
- Wearing only burlap sacks
- Living in a cave with WiFi
- Eating nothing but plain toast
- Deleting all your apps
- Trading your car for a donkey

What Real Spiritual Living Is:
- Using stuff without being used by it
- Enjoying things without worship
- Living in balance
- Keeping priorities straight
- Making Heaven your main flex

The Daily Balance Check

Morning Priority Scan:
1. The Quick Reality Check
- Is your stuff owning you?
- Are possessions possessing you?
- Has Amazon become your idol?
- Is TikTok your spiritual guide? (Note: Your worth isn't in your wardrobe!)

2. The Balance Moves
- Enjoy things lightly
- Hold stuff loosely
- Keep God first (Revolutionary idea: You can have nice things without them having you!)

Action Time! (Because Balance Needs Practice)

Today's Real Missions:

☑☐ Enjoy something without obsessing ☑☐ Share something you love ☑☐ Put God before stuff ☑☐ Keep priorities straight

Emergency Material Reset:
When stuff starts taking over:
1. Check your priorities
2. Reset your focus
3. Remember what lasts
4. Keep eternal perspective (Note: You can't take your TikTok followers to heaven!)

Your Weekly Balance Challenge:
Monday: "The Priority Pro"
- Enjoy stuff without worship
- Keep God as the main thing (Yes, you can still like your phone)

Tuesday: "The Balance Boss"
- Use things without being used
- Keep heaven in view (While still looking fabulous!)

Practical Steps:
1. Right Now:
- Check your attachments
- Reset your focus
- Enjoy without excess
- Keep God first
2. Today:
- Use stuff wisely
- Share freely
- Live balanced
- Stay focused

Your Immediate Mission:
STOP READING AND:
1. Check one attachment
2. Share something you love
3. Put God first once
4. Keep eternal focus

Remember: Even Solomon had bling - he just knew Who gave it to him!

Extra Credit: Try being grateful for your stuff instead of obsessed with it. Game changer! ✨

P.S. - Jesus never said you can't have nice things; He just said don't let them have you!

Now go forth and live balanced! And remember: You can be on fleek AND on fire for God! 🔥

Bonus Challenge: Do something spiritual while still looking stylish. Yes, it's possible!

Key Truth Bombs:
- Material ≠ Evil
- Stuff = Tools not treasures
- Things = Gifts not gods
- Style can serve Spirit

Because sometimes you can rock Gucci while serving God - it's all about where your heart's at! 💖

Remember: God invented good stuff - He just doesn't want it to invent you! Keep that perspective fresh and your priorities fresher! 💫

(Note: If your Bible app is your most-used app, you're probably doing something right! 📱)

CopyRetry

L

rewrite NEXT CHAPTER of the Imitation of Christ. make sure it is funny and actionable. try not to be repetitive

Edit

Chapter 54: How to Tell if It's God or Just Your Late-Night Taco Cravings! 🌮

The "Is This Divine or Just Dinner?" Challenge

Think every random thought is a holy message? That every feeling is a spiritual sign? NOPE! Let's learn how to spot the difference between divine direction and that spicy burrito!

What People Think God's Voice Is:
- Random fortune cookie messages
- Every gut feeling ever
- Magic 8-ball responses
- Random song lyrics
- That weird dream about flying pickles

What Real Divine Guidance Is:
- Aligns with God's Word

- Brings actual peace
- Makes spiritual sense
- Stands the time test
- Survives the taco test

The Daily Discernment Check
Morning Motivation Scan:
1. The Quick Source Check
- Is this God or guacamole?
- Divine wisdom or digestion?
- Holy Spirit or hot sauce?
- Actual guidance or appetite? (Note: Not every stomach growl is a spiritual signal!)
2. The Wisdom Moves
- Check against Scripture
- Test your motivations
- Seek wise counsel (Pro tip: God rarely tells you to buy everything in Target)

Action Time! (Because Discernment Takes Practice)
Today's Real Missions:
☑☐ Check one "spiritual" thought ☑☐ Test one motivation ☑☐ Seek actual wisdom ☑☐ Make smart choices

Emergency Discernment Protocol:
When unsure if it's God:
1. Check the Bible
2. Ask wise people
3. Wait it out
4. Test the fruit (Note: God's voice rarely demands immediate Amazon purchases)

Your Weekly Wisdom Challenge:
Monday: "The Motive Master"
- Check your real reasons
- Test your impulses (Is it God or just good marketing?)

Tuesday: "The Divine Detective"
- Investigate inspirations
- Sort spiritual signals (Sometimes it's just the pizza talking)

Practical Steps:

1. Right Now:
- Check one "message"
- Test one motivation
- Seek real wisdom
- Wait patiently
2. Today:
- Compare with Scripture
- Ask wise friends
- Watch the results
- Stay discerning

Your Immediate Mission:
STOP READING AND:
1. Test one "divine" thought
2. Check Scripture once
3. Ask someone wise
4. Wait before acting

Remember: Even Jesus took 40 days to test stuff!
Extra Credit: Start a "Was It God or Just Gas?" journal. The results might surprise you! 📸
P.S. - God's voice usually doesn't tell you to max out your credit card (even for "spiritual" reasons)!
Now go forth and discern wisely! And remember: Not every random thought is a revelation! ☐
Bonus Challenge: Wait 24 hours before acting on any "divine inspiration" that costs money!
Key Truth Tests:
- Does it match Scripture?
- Would Jesus retweet it?
- Is it still true after coffee?
- Does it pass the wise friend test?

Because sometimes what feels like a spiritual download is just a food coma in disguise! ☐
Remember: God's guidance is usually more "love your neighbor" and less "buy those shoes"! Though sometimes He might guide you to do both - just check your motives! 👟

(Special Note: If your spiritual promptings always involve shopping, maybe check who's really sending those messages! 🛍️)

Chapter 55: How to Level Up Your Spirit When Your Human Side is Being Sus!

The "Holy vs Hungry" Challenge
Think your spiritual side and human side are in an eternal cage match? That being holy means your human side has to tap out? NOPE! Let's learn how to manage both without losing your mind!

What People Think Spiritual Growth Means:
- Never getting hangry again
- Floating above human needs
- Becoming immune to Netflix
- Transcending the need for tacos
- Achieving permanent zen mode

What Real Growth Actually Is:
- Managing both sides well
- Balancing spirit and body
- Making wise choices
- Understanding your drives
- Leveling up while staying human

The Daily Balance Check
Morning Reality Scan:
1. The Quick Human Check
- Is your spirit driving or your stomach?
- Are you actually hungry or just bored?
- Is this prayer time or nap time?
- Which side needs attention? (Note: Hangry isn't a spiritual gift!)
2. The Balance Moves
- Feed both sides appropriately
- Handle human needs wisely

- Nurture spiritual growth (Revolutionary idea: You can be spiritual AND need a snack!)

Action Time! (Because Both Sides Need Love)
Today's Real Missions:
☑☐ Meet one human need wisely ☑☐ Feed your spirit actively
☑☐ Make balanced choices ☑☐ Level up both sides

Emergency Balance Protocol:
When sides conflict:
1. Check basic needs
2. Handle physical stuff
3. Address spiritual needs
4. Find healthy balance (Note: Sometimes the most spiritual thing is taking a nap!)

Your Weekly Growth Challenge:
Monday: "The Whole Person"
- Care for both sides
- Balance needs wisely (Yes, lunch breaks can be holy)

Tuesday: "The Level Upper"
- Grow spiritually
- Handle physically (Multitask: Pray while exercising!)

Practical Steps:
1. Right Now:
- Check both sides
- Meet real needs
- Make wise choices
- Stay balanced
2. Today:
- Handle human stuff
- Feed your spirit
- Keep growing
- Stay whole

Your Immediate Mission:
STOP READING AND:
1. Check your actual needs
2. Feed both sides
3. Make balanced choices
4. Keep growing wisely

Remember: Jesus took naps AND raised the dead!
Extra Credit: Try praying AFTER eating - you might hear God better when you're not hangry! 🍕
P.S. - Your body is a temple, but temples need maintenance! Now go forth and level up! And remember: Being spiritual doesn't mean ignoring your humanity!
Bonus Challenge: Do something spiritual while taking care of your human side!
Key Truth Bombs:
- Spirit needs food
- Body needs care
- Both sides matter
- Balance beats burnout

Because sometimes the most godly thing you can do is eat a sandwich and take a nap! ☐
Remember: God made both your spirit AND your need for pizza - He gets it! 🍕
(Special Note: Keep snacks in your prayer closet. Sometimes communion with God goes better with cookies! 🍪)

Chapter 56: How to Follow Jesus Without Becoming Weird About It!

The "Cool Christian Without the Cringe" Challenge

Think following Jesus means speaking in thee's and thou's? Wearing sandals year-round? NOPE! Let's learn how to walk with Jesus while keeping your actual personality!

What People Think Following Jesus Means:
- Speaking Christian-ese
- Posting Bible verses 24/7
- Making every conversation about church
- Becoming allergic to fun
- Only listening to worship music

What Real Following Actually Is:
- Being authentically Christian
- Living real faith daily
- Making Jesus look good
- Being salt AND lit
- Keeping it real with God

The Daily Discipleship Check

Morning Reality Scan:
1. The Quick Faith Check
   - Are you being real or religious?
   - Following Jesus or following trends?
   - Living faith or playing church?
   - Being authentic or awkward? (Note: Jesus was cool enough without our help!)
2. The Real Moves
   - Live authentic faith
   - Make Jesus attractive
   - Keep it genuine (Mind-blow: You can love Jesus AND be normal!)

Action Time! (Because Faith Needs Feet)

Today's Real Missions:

☑☐ Be genuinely Christian ☑☐ Make faith look good ☑☐ Live real devotion ☑☐ Keep it authentic

Emergency Authenticity Reset:

When getting too religious:
1. Check your realness
2. Drop the church voice
3. Be actually faithful
4. Stay genuine (Note: God gave you YOUR personality for a reason!)

Your Weekly Real Faith Challenge:
Monday: "The Authentic Awesome"
- Live real faith
- Keep your personality (Jesus likes the real you!)

Tuesday: "The Genuine Guide"
- Show others real faith
- Make Jesus look good (Without the weird church laugh)

Practical Steps:
1. Right Now:
- Be authentically you
- Live real faith
- Drop religious acts
- Stay genuine
2. Today:
- Keep it real
- Love Jesus normally
- Show true faith
- Stay yourself

Your Immediate Mission:
STOP READING AND:
1. Drop one fake religious thing
2. Be genuinely faithful
3. Make faith attractive
4. Stay authentically you

Remember: Jesus hung out with normal people!

Extra Credit: Have a normal conversation about faith without using "blessed" or "just" every other word! 😊

P.S. - If your faith makes others uncomfortable, you might be doing it wrong!

Now go forth and be real! And remember: You can love Jesus without becoming a different species!

Bonus Challenge: Show someone that Christians can be cool without trying too hard!

Key Truth Bombs:
- Real > Religious
- Authentic > Artificial
- Genuine > Fake
- Your personality isn't a sin

Because sometimes the best witness is just being a normal person who loves Jesus!

Remember: God made you unique - don't cover that up with a fake spiritual personality! ✨

(Special Note: It's okay if your testimony doesn't involve dramatic background music and slow-motion scenes! ♪)

Chapter 57: How to Bounce Back When You've Face-Planted in Life!

The "Epic Fail Recovery Guide" Challenge

Think messing up means game over? That one fail defines you? NOPE! Let's learn how to turn your fails into comebacks that even Rocky would applaud!

What People Think Recovery Means:
- Living in eternal shame
- Moving to a new country
- Changing your name
- Becoming a hermit
- Never showing your face again

What Real Recovery Is:
- Getting back up stronger
- Learning from face-plants
- Making epic comebacks
- Turning fails into fuel
- Becoming fail-proof funny

The Daily Bounce-Back Check

Morning Recovery Scan:
1. The Quick Fail Check
- Are you still face-down?
- Stuck in shame mode?
- Ready for a comeback?
- Learning anything yet? (Note: Even Peter denied Jesus and still became a rock star!)
2. The Comeback Moves
- Own your oops
- Learn your lesson
- Plan your rise (Plot twist: Your biggest fail could be your best story!)

Action Time! (Because Face-Plants Need Follow-Through)
Today's Recovery Missions:
☑☐ Face one fail honestly ☑☐ Learn one lesson ☑☐ Make one comeback plan ☑☐ Help someone else up

Emergency Recovery Protocol:
When failure hits hard:
1. Acknowledge the face-plant
2. Find the funny
3. Extract the lesson
4. Plan the comeback (Note: God's grace has better coverage than your mistakes!)

Your Weekly Bounce-Back Challenge:
Monday: "The Fail Forward"
- Own your stumbles
- Plan your jumps (Every saint has a past, every sinner has a future!)

Tuesday: "The Grace Chase"
- Accept forgiveness
- Spread recovery hope (Your mess can become your message)

Practical Steps:
1. Right Now:
- Face your fail
- Find the lesson
- Plan recovery

- Keep moving
2. Today:
- Stay humble
- Keep learning
- Help others
- Move forward

Your Immediate Mission:
STOP READING AND:
1. Own one mistake
2. Learn one lesson
3. Make one plan
4. Take one step

Remember: David's biggest fail became a Psalm!
Extra Credit: Share your fail story to help someone else (once it's funny, not while crying!) 😊
P.S. - If God can use Jonah after a whale incident, He can use you after whatever that was!
Now go forth and bounce back! And remember: It's not about how many times you fall, it's about how many times you get back up (and how good your recovery dance is)!
Bonus Challenge: Turn your most embarrassing fail into your best leadership lesson!
Key Truth Bombs:
- Falls aren't final
- Fails aren't fatal
- Grace is greater
- Comebacks are cooler

Because sometimes your biggest failures are just setups for your greatest testimonies! 💥
Remember: In God's hands, your mess becomes your message, your test becomes your testimony, and your fail becomes your fuel! 🚀
(Special Note: Keep some emergency chocolate for recovery days. Jesus never said you had to bounce back without snacks! 🍫)

Chapter 58: How to Trust God When Life Makes Zero Sense!

The "When God's Plan Looks Like a Modern Art Painting" Challenge

Think understanding God means having all the answers? That faith needs everything explained? NOPE! Let's learn how to trust when life looks like a puzzle with missing pieces!

What People Think Faith Means:
- Having a spiritual GPS for everything
- Getting divine text messages daily
- Understanding every "why"
- Seeing the whole game plan
- Getting heavenly spoiler alerts

What Real Trust Is:
- Rolling with God's mystery
- Vibing with the unknown
- Staying cool in confusion
- Dancing in the dark
- Trusting the plot twists

The Daily Mystery Check

Morning Trust Scan:
1. The Quick Reality Check
- Are you trying to solve God?
- Playing spiritual detective?
- Demanding all the answers?
- Fighting the mystery? (Note: Even angels don't know everything!)
2. The Trust Moves
- Accept the unknown
- Roll with mystery
- Find peace in questions (Plot twist: Not knowing is part of growing!)

Action Time! (Because Faith Needs Steps)

Today's Trust Missions:

☑☐ Accept one mystery ☑☐ Trust one unknown ☑☐ Find peace in questions ☑☐ Roll with God's plot

Emergency Mystery Protocol:
When confusion hits:
1. Embrace the unknown
2. Trust the Author
3. Enjoy the story
4. Keep moving forward (Note: Not even Google knows everything!)

Your Weekly Trust Challenge:
Monday: "The Mystery Master"
- Accept what's unclear
- Trust what's unknown (God's got better plot twists than Netflix)

Tuesday: "The Faith Flipper"
- Turn questions into trust
- Convert confusion to peace (Better than any home renovation show!)

Practical Steps:
1. Right Now:
- Accept one unknown
- Trust one mystery
- Find one peace point
- Keep walking
2. Today:
- Roll with questions
- Trust the process
- Stay peaceful
- Keep faithful

Your Immediate Mission:
STOP READING AND:
1. List one mystery you'll accept
2. Choose one thing to trust
3. Find peace in confusion
4. Take one faith step

Remember: Job never got his "why" but he got more of God!
Extra Credit: Make a "Things I Don't Need to Figure Out" list.
Warning: May be longer than expected!

P.S. - If you understood everything about God, He'd be too small to worship!

Now go forth and trust! And remember: Sometimes not knowing the plan IS the plan!

Bonus Challenge: Find joy in one thing you don't understand!

Key Truth Bombs:
- Mystery isn't misery
- Questions aren't failures
- Confusion can be cool
- Trust beats understanding

Because sometimes the best part of the story is not knowing what comes next! 📖

Remember: God wrote the universe - pretty sure He can handle your plot twist! ✨

(Special Note: Keep chocolate handy for days when God's ways are extra mysterious. Faith flows better with sugar! 🍫)

Chapter 59: How to Make God Your Ultimate Support System Without Being Clingy!

The "God's Got You Without the Codependency" Challenge

Think trusting God means spamming heaven's hotline? That faith means spiritual velcro? NOPE! Let's learn how to lean on God while keeping your cool!

What People Think God-Dependence Means:
- Praying about which socks to wear
- Calling the prayer hotline hourly
- Having a spiritual crisis over breakfast choices
- Never making any decisions alone
- Becoming a professional worrier

What Real Trust Actually Is:
- Having solid faith without the freak-out
- Walking with God like a boss
- Making wise moves with confidence
- Living secure in His support

- Being strong because of His backup

The Daily Trust Check
Morning Connection Scan:
1. The Quick Faith Check
- Are you trusting or stressing?
- Leaning or collapsing?
- Walking or worrying?
- Growing or groveling? (Note: God's your Father, not your panic button!)
2. The Confidence Moves
- Trust without trembling
- Walk without wobbling
- Live without freaking (Mind-blow: You can trust God AND have it together!)

Action Time! (Because Faith Needs Swagger)
Today's Trust Missions:
☑☐ Make one confident move ☑☐ Trust without trembling
☑☐ Walk in wisdom ☑☐ Live with assurance

Emergency Faith Protocol:
When doubt creeps in:
1. Remember His track record
2. Recall His promises
3. Stand in confidence
4. Move forward (Note: God's got better backup than your phone's cloud storage!)

Your Weekly Faith Challenge:
Monday: "The Trust Warrior"
- Walk tall in faith
- Stand firm in grace (Like a spiritual superhero, but normal)

Tuesday: "The Confidence Captain"
- Live bold in trust
- Move strong in faith (Without the spiritual superiority complex)

Practical Steps:
1. Right Now:
- Choose confidence

- Pick trust
- Walk tall
- Move forward
2. Today:
- Live assured
- Trust wisely
- Stand strong
- Keep growing

Your Immediate Mission:
STOP READING AND:
1. Make one bold move
2. Choose one trust point
3. Take one confident step
4. Walk in assurance

Remember: Moses split a sea but started with a stick!
Extra Credit: Make a decision without second-guessing it seventeen times! ☐
P.S. - God's got better plans than your backup plans to your backup plans!
Now go forth and trust like a boss! And remember: You can be confident AND dependent on God!
Bonus Challenge: Do something scary while trusting God (No, asking your crush out doesn't count as a spiritual exercise!)
Key Truth Bombs:
- Faith has swagger
- Trust has backbone
- Confidence comes from above
- God's got better insurance than State Farm

Because sometimes the strongest faith looks like calm confidence rather than constant crisis! 💪
Remember: God didn't give you a spirit of fear, but of power, love, and a sound mind (that means you can actually use it!)
(Special Note: Your faith can be solid without being solemn - pretty sure Jesus laughed too! ☺)

Book 4, Chapter 1: How to Meet Jesus Without Fainting!

The "Meeting the Ultimate VIP" Guide

Listen up, future saints! We're about to talk about something more epic than any Marvel finale - receiving Jesus Himself! This isn't like meeting your favorite YouTuber; this is THE moment where heaven meets earth.

The Sacred Part (Keeping It Reverent) 🙏

The Holy Eucharist is where the infinite God of the universe makes Himself present under the appearance of bread and wine. This is no symbolic gesture or spiritual metaphor - this is Jesus Christ, body, blood, soul, and divinity, coming to meet you personally.

This sacred mystery, where the King of Kings comes to dwell with us, deserves our deepest reverence and most profound respect. When we approach the altar, we're literally approaching the throne of grace, where Jesus waits to meet us with infinite love.

Now, Let's Talk About Our Part (Where the Fun Begins) 😊

What People Think Preparation Means:

Floating to church on a cloud of holiness
Having achieved perfect enlightenment
Never having thought a single grumpy thought
Being surrounded by visible halos
Hearing angels sing when you wake up

What It Actually Means:

Showing up with a clean heart (and hopefully clean socks)
Being genuinely sorry for that time you blamed your sister for eating the last cookie
Making peace with your siblings (yes, even THAT one)
Actually paying attention during Mass (scrolling Twitter doesn't count)
Remembering you're meeting Jesus (not just getting a spiritual drive-through)

The Pre-Jesus Meeting Checklist

Spiritual Prep:
Hit the confession booth before the big meet
Clear your spiritual browser history
Make peace with your enemies (including your brother who borrowed your charger and lost it)
Clean your heart (like Mom makes you clean your room, but better)
Physical Prep:
Fast for one hour (no, sleep time doesn't count!)
Dress appropriately (superhero pajamas are for home only)
Arrive early (yes, this means setting an alarm)
Remember it's Jesus, not a casual hangout
Emergency Protocol for Meeting Jesus:
When approaching the altar:
Remember who you're meeting
Keep it reverent
Don't trip (but if you do, play it cool)
Focus on the sacred moment (Note: This is NOT the time for your victory dance)
The "Don't Do This" List:
Don't treat it like a spiritual drive-through
Don't rush through your prayers
Don't check your phone during Communion
Don't fist-bump Jesus (tempting, but no)
Don't treat the altar like a race track
The "Actually Do This" List:
Approach with reverence (like meeting a king, because you are!)
Say "Amen" like you mean it (not like you're falling asleep)
Take a moment for thanksgiving (longer than a TikTok video)
Remember this is literally Jesus (more important than any celebrity)
Practical Steps for Not Freaking Out:
Breathe (Jesus likes it when you're conscious)
Focus (this is bigger than any game finale)
Remember He loves you (even with your bed still unmade)
Be present in the moment (Instagram can wait)
After Meeting Jesus:

Take time to say thanks
Actually spend time in prayer
Let His presence change you
Try to be nice to your siblings (the true test of grace)
Remember: This is the most epic meeting of your life - way bigger than any meet-and-greet with your favorite YouTuber!

Final Thoughts:
The Eucharist is where infinite God meets finite us - it's like the ultimate crossover episode, but holy. Treat it with the reverence it deserves, but don't be so nervous you forget it's about love.

Pro Tips:
If you're nervous, remember Jesus invented chill
It's okay to be excited (just keep it reverent)
This is better than any VIP pass
Your guardian angel is probably facepalming at your wandering thoughts (but Jesus loves you anyway)
Because sometimes the most incredible things happen in the most ordinary places - like Jesus, King of the Universe, coming to meet you at your local church!
Remember: He's not just any VIP - He's the Very Important Person who created VIPs! Show some respect, but remember He's also the one who loves you enough to meet you where you are (even with your questionable fashion choices and dragon breath)!
Now go forth and meet Jesus like the future saint you are! (Just remember to actually prepare first!) 🙇✨

Book 4, Chapter 2: God's Ultimate Plot Twist - The Greatest Love Story Ever!

The "God's Love is Way Bigger Than Your Phone's Storage" Guide

Alright future saints, gather 'round! We're about to dive into something more mind-blowing than any season finale - how God shows His epic love through the Sacrament. And trust me, this makes your favorite love story look like a kindergarten crush!

The Sacred Part (Ultimate Reverence Time) 🙏

In the Most Holy Sacrament of the Altar, God demonstrates the most profound act of love imaginable. Here, the Creator of the universe, the One who scattered stars like glitter and shaped galaxies like clay, humbles Himself to become present under the appearance of bread and wine. This isn't just any gift - this is God literally giving Himself to us, holding nothing back, showing a love so vast it makes the ocean look like a kiddie pool.

In this Sacred Mystery, Jesus proves that love isn't just a word - it's an action so radical it defies human understanding. He gives us His very Body and Blood, Soul and Divinity, making the infinite accessible to the finite, the eternal touchable to the temporal.

Now, Let's Break Down This Divine Love Language 😊

What People Think God's Love Looks Like:

Constant perfect hair days
Never losing at video games
Finding money in your old jeans
Getting extra fries at the bottom of the bag
Your siblings being mysteriously quiet

What God's Love Actually Is:

Literally becoming bread to feed your soul
The ultimate "I'd do anything for you" move
Breaking the laws of physics to be with you
Making forever love fit into a moment

The original "greater love has no one than this"
The "Mind = Blown" List
Things That Show Less Commitment Than the Eucharist:
Your New Year's resolutions
Your promise to clean your room
Your "forever" friendship bracelets
Your dedication to your diet
Your plan to wake up early tomorrow
Things God Does in the Eucharist:
Breaks the laws of physics
Proves love > logic
Makes infinity portable
Turns bread into Himself
Outdoes every love story ever written
Emergency Perspective Protocol:
When you're not feeling the wonder:
Remember who's really present
Think about what's actually happening
Consider the love involved
Pick your jaw up off the floor (Note: Proper response includes mild brain explosion)
The "This is Actually Happening" Reality Check:
God invented galaxies but wants to meet you
The One who crafted DNA comes as bread
Eternal love becomes bite-sized
Heaven touches earth (without earth exploding)
Jesus says "I'll never ghost you" and means it
Proof God's Got Game:
Makes Himself accessible 24/7
Comes to your neighborhood
Doesn't require a VIP pass
Always has time for you
Never leaves you on read
When You Really Think About It:
This is more impressive than:
Any superhero transformation
Your favorite plot twist

That time you actually found matching socks
When Mom found her keys immediately
Getting all green lights on the way to school

The Love Language Stats:
God's Love Shown Through:
Words of Affirmation: The Bible
Acts of Service: Creation
Receiving Gifts: The Eucharist
Quality Time: Always Present
Physical Touch: Literally becomes bread

Final Epic Truth Bombs:
Remember:
This love story makes Romeo and Juliet look like amateurs
God's flex game is stronger than any influencer
The ultimate "I'll be there for you" wasn't written by The Rembrandts
Heaven's idea of a perfect date is every Mass
Jesus invented commitment before it was cool
Because sometimes the most epic love stories aren't on Netflix - they're happening at your local church!

Pro Tips for Appreciating This Divine Plot Twist:
Consider the commitment level:
Your average relationship: "I'll text you later"
God in the Eucharist: "I'll literally become bread for you"
Think about the availability:
Your best friend: "I'll be there in 5 minutes"
Jesus: "I'm already here, in every tabernacle, always"
Ponder the dedication:
Regular love: "I'd climb mountains for you"
God's love: "I'll break the laws of physics and time for you"
Remember: This is the ultimate "I love you" - no emoji required!
God's love in the Eucharist makes even your most dramatic declaration of love look like a casual "sup"!
Now go forth and appreciate this divine love story! Just try not to faint when you realize how epic it actually is!

Book 4, Chapter 3: Why Frequent Communion is Better Than Your Social Media Feed!

The "More Jesus, Less Drama" Guide

Listen up, future saints! We're about to talk about why going to Communion frequently is more essential than checking your notifications. (Spoiler alert: One feeds your soul, the other just tells you what Karen had for lunch.)

The Sacred Part (Maximum Reverence Mode) 🙏

The Holy Eucharist is the most profound encounter possible between God and humanity. In this Most Blessed Sacrament, Jesus Christ offers Himself as spiritual nourishment for our souls. Each reception of Holy Communion is a direct, personal encounter with the Living God, who strengthens us, purifies us, and transforms us more deeply into His image. This sacred gift, far from being a rare privilege, is meant to be our regular spiritual sustenance, drawing us ever closer to the heart of God.

Now, Let's Talk About Frequency (Where The Fun Begins) 😊

What People Think "Regular Communion" Means:

Once a year (like updating your phone)
Christmas and Easter (spiritual tourist mode)
When Grandma makes you go
After major life disasters
When you need divine backup for exams

What it Should Actually Be:

As often as properly prepared
Regular as your pizza cravings
Frequent as your social media checks
Consistent as your gaming schedule
More common than your TikTok scrolls

The "But I'm Not Worthy" Response Guide

Common Excuses:

"I'm not holy enough" (Neither was literally anyone else)
"I messed up too much" (That's literally why He's there)

"I'm not feeling it" (Neither is your workout, but you still need it)
"I'm too busy" (Busier than God who runs the universe?)
"I'll go when I'm better" (That's like saying you'll take medicine when you're healthy)

Emergency Reality Check Protocol:
When skipping Communion because you're "not worthy":
Remember nobody is "worthy"
That's the whole point
Jesus picks you anyway
Stop making excuses (Note: Your guardian angel is probably facepalming right now)

The "Spiritual Food vs. Regular Food" Comparison:
Regular Meals:
Three times daily
Need physical strength
Gets boring eventually
Lots of dishes to wash
Sometimes causes food coma
Spiritual Meals (Communion):
As often as possible
Gives eternal strength
Never gets old
No cleanup required
Causes spiritual awakening

Why Frequent Communion Makes Sense:
Physical vs. Spiritual Logic:
You wouldn't skip meals for a month
Your soul needs food more than your body
Spiritual hangry is worse than regular hangry
God's drive-through is always open
The Benefits Package:
Better than any gym membership
More lasting than energy drinks
Healthier than your vitamin gummies
More effective than your skincare routine

The "How Often" Decision Tree:

Are you:
Breathing? ✓
In a state of grace? ✓
Properly prepared? ✓ Then why aren't you going?

Pro Tips for Regular Reception:
Preparation Game:
Confession is your spiritual shower
Prayer is your soul's pre-game
Mass is your heavenly workout
Communion is your divine protein shake
Frequency Goals:
Aim for more often than you check Instagram
Try to beat your Snapchat streak
Make it more regular than your gaming sessions
More frequent than your snack breaks

Ultimate Truth Bombs:
Remember:
Jesus isn't a once-a-year relative you visit
Your soul needs food more than your phone needs charging
Grace > Gaming
Communion > Social Media
Divine Presence > Instagram Presence

The Real MVP Stats:
What You Get From Regular Communion:
Spiritual gains
Divine downloads
Grace upgrades
Soul strength
Eternal buffs
What You Get From Skipping:
Spiritual weakness
Soul hunger
Missed opportunities
Weaker defenses
Lower grace stats

Final Boss Wisdom:
Think about it:

You wouldn't go weeks without food
You wouldn't skip charging your phone
You wouldn't miss season updates in your game
So why skip spiritual power-ups?
Remember: This is literally God offering Himself as soul food!
He's like, "Here's infinite grace, just show up!" And we're like, "Nah, gotta check my streaks." 📱♂️📱
Now go forth and receive frequently! Just remember:
Proper preparation required
No spiritual sleeping
Actually pay attention
Jesus > TikTok
P.S. - Your soul's notification: "Divine food available. Don't leave Jesus on read!"
Because sometimes the most important daily bread isn't the one in your sandwich! 🥖✨

Book 4, Chapter 4: The Ultimate Power-Up: Holy Communion's Epic Bonus Pack!

The "Better Than Any Legendary Drop" Guide

Hold onto your prayer books, future saints! We're about to explore the most epic loot box in history - the incredible gifts you get from devout Communion. And trust me, this beats any rare item drop you've ever scored!

The Sacred Part (Deep Reverence Time) 🙏

In the Most Holy Eucharist, our Lord Jesus Christ bestows upon us gifts of incomprehensible value and eternal significance. With each devout reception, He pours forth graces that transform our souls, strengthen our spirits, and draw us deeper into divine life. This sacred exchange, where God Himself becomes our spiritual nourishment, brings with it treasures that no earthly wealth could ever match. Each Holy Communion is a moment of profound union with our Creator, carrying with it graces that ripple into eternity.

Now Let's Break Down These Divine Drops (The Fun Part) 🎮

What People Think Communion Gives You:

Instant angel wings
Automatic halo activation
Immediate immunity to little brother attacks
Perfect homework completion powers
Suddenly speaking in King James English

What You Actually Get (Way Better):

Divine strength (better than any energy drink)
Spiritual shield upgrades
Soul-level power-ups
Heavenly help packages
Grace-based growth spurts

The Divine Gift Guide (No Returns Necessary)
Level 1: Immediate Power-Ups

Temptation Resistance Boost

Like having a spiritual force field
Works better than Mom's "just ignore it"
Actually helps you be nice to siblings
Peace Package
Calmer than a sloth on vacation
More peaceful than your sleeping cat
Better than any chill pill
Level 2: Character Upgrades
Patience Points
Even with that one annoying classmate
During your sister's flute practice
While waiting for Mom in Target
Kindness Boosts
Helps you share the last cookie
Makes you consider others first
Might even make you nice to your brother
The "You Can't Buy This Stuff" Collection:
Things Money Can Buy:
New phone
Latest gaming console
Cool sneakers
Fancy snacks
Premium subscriptions
Things Only Communion Gives:
Eternal life upgrades
Divine friendship status
Heavenly help access
Soul-level improvements
Infinite grace packages
Emergency Gift Reception Protocol:
When receiving these epic gifts:
Actually pay attention
Be genuinely thankful
Use them wisely
Don't waste them on silly stuff (Note: Your guardian angel is keeping score!)
The "Better Than Amazon Prime" Benefits:

Delivery Speed:
Amazon: Next day
Communion: Instant divine download
Package Contents:
Regular mail: Stuff you'll forget next week
Communion: Eternal treasures
Shipping Cost:
Normal packages: $$$
Divine packages: Just show up prepared

Pro Tips for Maximum Gift Reception:
Preparation Matters:
Clean your soul (Confession)
Update your spiritual software (Prayer)
Clear your cache (Forgive others)
Make space for new downloads (Humility)
Reception Attitude:
Be more excited than Christmas morning
Show more interest than in your phone
Pay better attention than to your favorite show
Be more grateful than for free pizza

The "You're Getting WHAT?" Reality Check:
Consider This:
God literally gives Himself
Heaven touches earth
Eternal meets temporal
Divine meets human
Infinite fits in finite
And you're worried about your Instagram likes? ☐

Final Boss Wisdom:
Remember:
These gifts are better than any birthday haul
This power-up beats any game upgrade
These benefits outlast any subscription
This download is more important than any app update
Because sometimes the best gifts don't come in boxes, don't need batteries, and won't be obsolete next month!

The Ultimate Perspective:

Think about it:
You get excited about game rewards
You celebrate birthday presents
You love surprise deliveries
But THIS is literally God giving Himself!
Now go forth and receive these gifts like they're better than a new iPhone (because they are)! Just remember:
Proper preparation required
Actually appreciate what you're getting
Use the gifts wisely
Don't forget to say thanks
P.S. - If you're not excited about these gifts, you might need to check your spiritual WiFi connection!
Because sometimes the most epic loot drops happen at the communion rail! ✝️🙏

Book 4, Chapter 5: Why Being a Priest is More Epic Than Being a Superhero!

The "Ultimate Sacred Power" Guide

Alright future saints, buckle up! We're about to explore why priests have more power than any Marvel character (and yes, that includes Thor with his hammer!)

The Sacred Part (Ultimate Reverence Zone) 🙏

The dignity of the priesthood is a mystery of profound reverence. Through ordination, God grants these chosen men the sacred power to transform bread and wine into the actual Body and Blood of Christ. This supernatural ability, this divine commission, elevates the priesthood to a dignity that surpasses even that of angels. In the Most Holy Sacrament of the Altar, priests act in persona Christi, literally standing in the place of

Christ Himself, wielding a power that heaven itself regards with awe.

Now Let's Break Down The Priest Power Rankings 🌍

What People Think Priests Do:
Give long homilies
Tell kids to be quiet in church
Wear fancy robes
Master the art of incense swinging
Professional prayer warrior

What Priests Actually Do:
Transform bread into LITERAL JESUS
Channel heaven to earth
Wield divine power
Fight spiritual battles
Bridge infinity and time

The "Better Than Superhero Powers" List

Superhero vs. Priest Powers:
Superman
Can fly
Has super strength
Shoots laser eyes BUT CAN'T: Turn bread into Jesus
Doctor Strange
Does magic
Bends reality
Opens portals BUT CAN'T: Forgive sins
Thor
Controls lightning
Has a cool hammer
Lives for thousands of years BUT CAN'T: Bring heaven to earth

Emergency Priest Appreciation Protocol:
When you think priests aren't cool:
Remember they can turn bread into Jesus
Think about their sin-forgiving powers
Consider their heaven-opening abilities
Realize they're spiritual superheroes (Note: Your guardian angel agrees)

The "Cooler Than Your Average Job" Comparison:

Regular Cool Jobs:
Astronaut (goes to space)
Video Game Designer (makes virtual worlds)
Professional Athlete (wins games)
Movie Star (pretends to be cool)
Priest's Job:
Brings God to Earth
Opens heaven's gates
Fights actual spiritual battles
Has divine authority

Why Priests Are More Epic Than You Think:
Office Hours:
Regular Job: 9-5
Priest: On call for God 24/7
Job Benefits:
Regular Job: Health insurance, 401k
Priest: Eternal rewards package
Work Uniform:
Regular Job: Business casual
Priest: Sacred vestments (spiritual armor)

The "Not Your Average Power Level" Chart:
Powers They Don't Have:
Can't fly physically
Don't shoot laser beams
Can't read minds
No super strength
Powers They Actually Have:
Can forgive sins
Transform bread into Jesus
Open heaven's gates
Channel divine grace

Pro Tips for Priest Appreciation:
Remember they're:
Spiritual warriors
Divine channels
Heaven's ambassadors
God's chosen ones

Show respect by:
Not sleeping during homilies
Actually saying thank you
Praying for them
Remembering they're human too

The "Cooler Than You Realized" Truth Bombs:
Think About It:
They can do what angels can't
They handle what heaven reveres
They wield power beyond comprehension
They bring God to Earth daily

Final Boss Wisdom:
Remember:
Priests > Superheroes
Sacred power > Super power
Divine authority > Earthly authority
Spiritual battles > Physical battles
Because sometimes the most powerful people don't wear capes - they wear stoles!

The Reality Check:
Consider:
Spider-Man: Swings through city
Priest: Swings thurible, brings down heaven
Iron Man: Has cool armor
Priest: Has sacred vestments that actually mean something
Batman: Fights crime
Priest: Fights literal evil

Now go forth and appreciate your local spiritual superhero! Just remember:
They're still human
They need prayer
They appreciate thanks
They probably still like normal stuff

P.S. - Next time you see your priest, remember he has more power than the entire Avengers team combined!

Because sometimes the most incredible powers aren't the ones that make the biggest explosion, but the ones that transform souls! ✨🙇
(Just don't ask them to prove their powers by turning water into wine at parties - that's not how this works! 😊)

Book 4, Chapter 6: How to Get Ready for Holy Communion Without Having a Spiritual Panic Attack!

The "Divine Meet-Up Prep" Guide

Okay future saints, let's talk about preparing to meet Jesus in the Eucharist! This is bigger than prepping for picture day, more important than getting ready for a video game tournament, and way more significant than your plan to finally clean your room!

The Sacred Part (Maximum Reverence Engaged) 🙇

The Most Holy Eucharist requires our most profound preparation. This sacred encounter with our Lord Jesus Christ demands a heart made ready through prayer, confession, and sincere contrition. We must approach this divine mystery with the deepest reverence, understanding that we come before the King of Kings, truly present under the appearance of bread and wine. Our preparation should reflect the magnificent reality that we will receive God Himself.

Now Let's Talk Prep Work (The Fun Part) 😊
What People Think Preparation Means:
Levitating in prayer for three days
Memorizing the entire Bible
Never having a single bad thought
Achieving monk-level tranquility
Becoming allergic to fun

What Real Prep Actually Is:
Getting your heart ready (and yes, brush your teeth)
Making peace with everyone (even your annoying sibling)
Clearing your conscience (confession is key)
Focusing your mind (harder than it sounds)
Actually paying attention (seriously, try it)
The "Getting Ready" Checklist
Spiritual Hygiene:
Soul Check
Like checking your teeth for spinach
But checking your soul for sin
Way more important than your hair
Attitude Adjustment
Less "ugh, church again"
More "wow, meeting Jesus!"
Think less Eeyore, more joy
Focus Setting
Turn down brain static
Turn up spiritual antenna
Results may vary
Emergency Preparation Protocol:
When you're panicking about being ready:
Take a deep breath
Hit the confession box
Say some actual prayers
Remember who loves you (Note: Stress-eating communion hosts is NOT preparation)
The "Clean Up Your Act" Guide:
Physical vs. Spiritual Clean-Up:
Room Cleaning:
Stuff under bed
Closet chaos
Mystery smells
Lost homework
Soul Cleaning:
Hit confession
Fix relationships

Drop bad habits
Find lost virtues
The Pre-Communion Countdown:
T-minus 24 hours:
Check conscience
Plan confession
Warn family you're trying to be nice
Practice looking reverent
T-minus 12 hours:
Start fasting
Set alarm (yes, really)
Choose church clothes
Pre-load peace mode
T-minus 1 hour:
Final attitude check
Phone in airplane mode
Brain in focus mode
Heart in receiving mode
The "Don't Do This" List:
Common Prep Fails:
Practicing your runway walk to communion
Planning your post-communion Instagram story
Treating it like a divine drive-through
Rehearsing your "I'm holy" face
Pro Tips for Real Preparation:
Mental Ready-Up:
Think about WHO you're meeting
Consider WHY you're there
Remember WHAT'S happening
Forget about your hair for five minutes
Heart Check Steps:
Are you actually sorry for stuff?
Have you forgiven that person?
Yes, even THAT person
Including your brother who lost your charger
The Ultimate Reality Check:
Remember:

You're meeting actual Jesus
This isn't a social event
Your soul matters more than your outfit
God sees through your "I'm totally paying attention" face
Final Boss Wisdom:
Think about it:
You prep more for a selfie
You practice more for games
You plan more for pizza
But this is LITERAL GOD
Now go forth and prepare properly! Just remember:
God wants you ready, not perfect
Preparation matters more than presentation
It's about your heart, not your hair
Your guardian angel can't do this for you
P.S. - If you put as much effort into spiritual prep as you do into your gaming setup, you'd be a saint by now!
Because sometimes the most important preparation isn't about what people see, but what God sees! ✨🙇
Extra Credit: Try preparing your soul as carefully as you prepare your social media posts. Results guaranteed to be more lasting! 😇

Book 4, Chapter 7: The Ultimate Soul Spring Cleaning Guide!

The "Checking Your Spiritual Closet" Manual

Alright future saints! Time to dive into something scarier than your room after a month of "I'll clean it tomorrow" - it's time for a conscience check! Don't worry, it's like a virus scan for your soul, just more effective and less annoying than those computer updates.

The Sacred Part (Deep Reverence Mode) 🙏

The examination of conscience before receiving the Most Holy Eucharist is a matter of profound spiritual importance. We must approach the Blessed Sacrament with hearts that have been carefully examined, cleansed through sincere contrition and confession, and prepared through genuine amendment of life. This sacred duty of self-examination helps ensure we receive our Lord with the reverence and purity He deserves.

Now Let's Deep Clean That Conscience! 😊

What People Think Examination Means:

Torturing yourself over every tiny mistake
Writing a 500-page autobiography of sins
Achieving perfect memory of every wrong thought
Becoming a professional self-critic
Turning into a guilt-powered superhero

What It Actually Is:

Honest soul inventory
Spiritual reality check
Divine truth-or-dare (minus the dare part)
Heart housekeeping
conscience cleanup crew

The "Soul Search" Survival Guide

Level 1: Basic Scan

Check Your Recent Downloads
What's been entering your mind?
Which websites did your eyes visit?
What apps is your soul running?

Virus Check
Scan for jealousy bugs
Look for pride malware
Check for attitude viruses
Level 2: Deep Clean
Relationship Status
Parents: Still honoring them?
Siblings: How many fights?
Friends: Any backstabbing?
God: Left on read?
The "Things We Conveniently Forget" List:
Common Memory "Glitches":
"I was BARELY lying"
"They deserved that comment"
"It was just a small cheat"
"Everyone else does it"
"The dog ate my homework" (Classic)
Emergency Memory Protocol:
When conscience checking:
Actually try to remember
Don't make excuses
Be brutally honest
Check all corners (Note: Your guardian angel has the receipts!)
The Great Soul Sort:
Organize By Category:
Thoughts:
Random brain chaos
Intentional mind mess
That thing you imagined doing to your brother
Words:
Things you shouldn't have said
Things you should have said
That comeback you're still proud of
Actions:
What you did
What you didn't do
What you pretended not to do

The "Don't Skip These" Checklist:
Common Cover-Ups:
"Borrowing" without asking
"Alternative facts" (lies)
"Just resting my eyes" in church
"I'll do it later" promises
Hidden Folders:
Secret attitudes
Private grudges
Stealth eye-rolls
Invisible complaints
Pro Tips for Thorough Searching:
Check Under The Spiritual Bed:
Dust bunnies of pride
Monster of laziness
Lost socks of charity
Missing homework of holiness
Look Behind The Heart's Couch:
Old grudges
Stale attitudes
Forgotten promises
That thing you said you'd fix
The Reality Check List:
Remember to Check:
Commandment compliance
Beatitude adherence
Golden Rule following
Actual effort made
Final Boss Wisdom:
Think About:
When was your last virus scan?
How's your spiritual storage?
Any corrupted files?
Need a divine debug?
Because sometimes your soul needs a cleanup more than your room! (Though maybe do both?)
The Ultimate Cleanup Motivation:

Consider:
God sees everything anyway
Your guardian angel is taking notes
Jesus is waiting to help
Grace works better than excuses
Now go forth and check that conscience! Just remember:
Be honest (God knows anyway)
Be thorough (no spiritual shortcuts)
Be sincere (actual sorry, not sorry-not-sorry)
Be ready to change (yes, for real this time)
P.S. - If you spent as much time checking your conscience as you do checking your social media, you'd probably be a saint by now!
Because sometimes the most important notifications are from your conscience! ✨🙏
(Note: Unlike your room, you can't just shove everything under the spiritual bed and call it clean! 😇)

Book 4, Chapter 8: The Great Trade Deal: Giving Up Everything for Everything!

Introduction: The Ultimate Exchange Program

Think you're good at trading? Made some epic Pokémon card swaps? Well, hold onto your holy water, because we're about to discuss the most epic trade in history - where Jesus offered Himself on the cross, and now invites us to join in this divine exchange program!

The Sacred Part (Deep Reverence Zone) 🙏
The supreme sacrifice of Christ on the cross represents the most profound act of love in all existence. In the Holy Eucharist, this sacrifice is made present to us in an unbloody manner. When we approach the altar, we're invited to unite our own self-

offering with Christ's perfect sacrifice. This sacred union calls us to surrender everything to Him who gave everything for us.

Part 1: What We're Trading

FROM US	FROM GOD
Our mess	His perfection
Our weakness	His strength
Our Netflix addiction	His eternal glory
Our meme collection	His divine wisdom
Our limited edition stuff	His infinite treasures

Part 2: The Great Misunderstandings

People Think Surrender Means:
Copy
- 🚫 Becoming a robot
- 🚫 Never having fun again
- 🚫 Living in a cave
- 🚫 Eating only bread and water
- 🚫 Deleting all your games

What It Actually Means:
Copy
- ✅ Finding real freedom
- ✅ Getting ultimate purpose
- ✅ Living your best life
- ✅ Experiencing true joy
- ✅ Playing on God's team

Part 3: The Investment Strategy

Short-Term Sacrifices:
That extra hour of sleep
Your favorite bad habit
That grudge you're nursing
Your "me first" attitude
Your carefully curated excuses

Eternal Returns:
Infinite happiness
Everlasting peace
Divine friendship

Eternal high score
Heavenly mansion

Part 4: Common Trading Mistakes

ERROR LOG:

Copy

ERROR 404: Full Commitment Not Found
ERROR 501: Trying to Keep Backup Plans
ERROR 303: Partial Surrender Attempted
ERROR 202: Terms & Conditions Not Read
ERROR 608: Still Playing Both Sides

Part 5: The Sacrifice Survival Guide

Step 1: Initial Offering

Start small (God appreciates the effort)
Be consistent (unlike your room cleaning)
Stay committed (better than your New Year's resolutions)

Step 2: Level Up Your Game

python

Copy

```
def daily_sacrifice():
    if feeling_lazy:
        get_up_anyway()
    if tempted:
        choose_better()
    if struggling:
        keep_going()
    return eternal_reward
```

Part 6: The Reality Check Quiz

Ask Yourself:
Am I trading temporary for eternal?
Is this upgrade worth the grind?
Have I read the divine user agreement?
Am I still keeping backup saves?

Part 7: The Divine Exchange Rate

WORLDLY CURRENCY	HEAVENLY VALUE
Instagram likes	Divine approval
Viral videos	Eternal glory

WORLDLY CURRENCY HEAVENLY VALUE

Temporary fame   Everlasting joy

Earthly treasures   Heavenly riches

Part 8: Warning Labels

⚠️ **CAUTION:**

Side effects may include increased joy

May result in unexpected peace

Could lead to eternal happiness

Might cause spontaneous acts of kindness

Warning: Grace is highly addictive

Part 9: The Fine Print

By accepting this offer you agree to:

Give up your own plans

Follow divine GPS

Accept heavenly upgrades

Join Team Jesus

Receive eternal benefits

Part 10: The Final Pitch

Remember:

"For what shall it profit a man, if he gain the whole world and lose his own soul?" (Ancient wisdom that hits harder than your mom's Wi-Fi restrictions)

Now go forth and make the trade! Just remember:

No takebacks necessary (God's deals are always better)

Full warranty included (grace coverage)

Eternal customer service (24/7 prayer line)

Satisfaction guaranteed (or your old sins back - just kidding!)

Because sometimes the best trades aren't on the stock market - they're at the altar!

And hey, if you're still unsure, remember this: Jesus traded heaven for a manger, a throne for a cross, and did it all for you. Your move, future saint! 😇✨

P.S. - Unlike your other trades, this one's definitely not a scam! Divine guarantee included! 🌟

Book 4, Chapter 9: How to Be God's Gift To Everyone (The Right Way!)

MISSION BRIEFING: Operation Total Gift Mode

Hey future saints! Ever get that awesome birthday gift and think, "I'm totally keeping this forever and never sharing!" Well, today we're learning about being a gift to others and giving God EVERYTHING. Yes, even your secret candy stash!

THE SERIOUS STUFF (Super Important - Pay Attention!)
In the Most Holy Eucharist, Jesus gives Himself completely to us as the perfect gift of love. This total self-giving shows us how we should offer ourselves and everything we have to God and others. When we bring our gifts to the altar, we're joining our small offerings to Christ's perfect sacrifice, making them way more awesome than they could be on their own.

MISSION OBJECTIVES: Becoming a Human Gift
LEVEL 1: STARTER GIFTS
Your time (yes, even when Fortnite is calling)
Your talents (more than just your epic gaming skills)
Your treasures (that candy bar won't last forever anyway)
LEVEL 2: ADVANCED GIVING
Your attitude (especially when Mom says "clean your room")
Your effort (more than just the bare minimum)
Your prayers (God likes those better than your wishlist)

SECRET AGENT TRAINING GUIDE
GIFT GIVING STATUS CHECK:
Copy
CURRENTLY HOARDING:
☐ Time for videos
☐ Energy for games
☐ Excuses for chores
☐ Snacks from siblings

SHOULD BE SHARING:
☐ Help with dishes

☐ Time with family
☐ Kindness to annoying people
☐ Last piece of pizza (the ultimate test)

FIELD OPERATIONS MANUAL
TOP SECRET MISSIONS:
Operation Clean Room
Without being asked (Mom might faint)
Actually finding the floor
Bonus points: Making your bed
Project Help Sibling
Even when they're annoying
Especially when they're annoying
Supreme challenge: Being nice about it
Mission Impossible: Share Snacks
The ultimate sacrifice
Yes, even the good ones
Double points for last cookie sharing

EQUIPMENT CHECK: What You Need
ESSENTIAL GEAR: 🎮 Self-control (harder than any game boss) 🌱 Good attitude (your secret weapon) ☐☐ Patience (your spiritual armor) ⚔☐ Kindness (your power move)

GIFT-GIVING POWER LEVELS
ROOKIE MOVES:
Sharing only when forced
Helping only if bribed
Praying only for stuff you want
LEGENDARY MOVES:
Giving your best, not leftovers
Helping without being caught
Praying for others first

COMMON MISSION FAILURES
AGENT ERROR REPORT:
Copy
ERROR #1: "But it's MINE!"
STATUS: Mission Compromised
FIX: Remember everything's from God anyway

ERROR #2: "I'll do it later..."
STATUS: Mission Delayed
FIX: Do it now, game later

ERROR #3: "They don't deserve it!"
STATUS: Mission Critical
FIX: Neither do you, but God's nice anyway

SPECIAL FORCES TRAINING

HOW TO LEVEL UP YOUR GIVING:
Start Small
Hold the door
Share a smile
Don't hog the bathroom
Build Up
Help with groceries
Teach someone something
Give up the comfy chair
Go Pro
Love your enemies
Share your best stuff
Be nice to your siblings (the ultimate challenge)

MISSION REWARDS

EARTHLY BENEFITS:
People actually like you
Parents trust you more
Less guilty conscience
More inner peace

HEAVENLY REWARDS:
Eternal high score
Divine appreciation
Heavenly treasure
God's epic "well done"

EMERGENCY PROTOCOLS

WHEN SELFISHNESS ATTACKS:
Remember God's gifts to you
Think of others first
Just do it anyway

Offer it up
FINAL MISSION BRIEFING
Remember Agent:
You can't outgive God
Everything good is a gift
Sharing multiplies joy
Being selfish = missing out
YOUR DAILY MISSION:
Find one thing to share
Help one person
Make one sacrifice
Give one compliment
Because sometimes being God's gift to everyone isn't about being perfect - it's about being perfectly willing to share!
SPECIAL NOTE TO AGENTS IN TRAINING:
Start with something easy
Build up your giving muscles
Keep practicing
Don't give up
And remember: Even Jesus shared His lunch with 5000 people - surely you can share your french fries! 🍟
END TRANSMISSION MISSION STATUS: ACTIVE YOUR CHOICE: ACCEPT OR DECLINE (But seriously, accept it - it's way better than being selfish!)

Book 4, Chapter 10: Why Skipping Communion is Like Missing Out on Free Legendary Loot!

DOWNLOADING DIVINE WISDOM...
██████████████████ 100%

THE SACRED STUFF (Pay Attention - This is Important!)
Holy Communion is the most precious gift Jesus left us - His own Body and Blood, Soul and Divinity. Choosing to skip this sacred feast without good reason is like turning down an invitation from the King of the Universe. The Eucharist is our spiritual food, strengthening our souls and keeping us connected to God in the most intimate way possible.

PLAYER'S GUIDE TO NOT MISSING OUT
COMMON EXCUSES VS REALITY:

EXCUSE	REALITY
"I'm too tired"	You stayed up till 2AM gaming
"I'm not worthy"	Nobody is - that's the point!
"Church is boring"	Meeting God > Your phone
"I'll go next week"	Said that last week too...

DAMAGE REPORT: What You Miss When You Skip
Level 1: Immediate Power-Ups Lost
Divine strength boost
Spiritual shield upgrades
Holy hit points
Grace power-ups

Level 2: Long-Term Debuffs
Weakened spiritual defense
Lower resistance to temptation
Decreased holy stats
Reduced divine connection

THE ATTENDANCE ACHIEVEMENT SYSTEM

🏆 NOOB: Shows up on Christmas and Easter 🏆 CASUAL: Monthly appearance 🏆 REGULAR: Weekly warrior 🏆 LEGENDARY: Never misses without reason

WARNING SIGNS YOU'RE MAKING BAD CHOICES
Copy
ALERT: Your spiritual battery is low!
WARNING: Connection to divine server weakening!
CAUTION: Soul needs recharging!
DANGER: Grace levels critically low!

HOW TO STAY IN THE GAME

Step 1: Pre-Game Prep
Set that alarm (yes, really)
Plan ahead (like you plan gaming sessions)
Get to bed on time (shocking, I know)
Remember why you're going

Step 2: Combat Laziness
python
Copy

```python
if feeling_lazy:
    remember_eternal_rewards()
    think_about_Jesus_sacrifice()
    get_up_anyway()
```

Step 3: Stay Motivated

TEMPORARY PAIN	ETERNAL GAIN
Early wake-up	Divine power-up
Missing cartoons	Meeting God
Less gaming time	More grace points
Actually paying attention	Leveling up spiritually

EPIC REWARDS FOR SHOWING UP
What You Get:
Actual Jesus (better than any legendary drop)
Divine grace (better than energy drinks)
Spiritual strength (better than power-ups)
Eternal rewards (better than high scores)

EMERGENCY MOTIVATION PROTOCOLS
When tempted to skip:

Remember Who you're missing
Think about what you're losing
Consider the eternal consequences
Just show up (80% of success!)
PRO GAMER TIPS
How to Make It:
Sunday Game Plan
Prepare Saturday night
Set multiple alarms
Have clothes ready
Plan your route
Power-Up Strategy
Get there early (yes, it's possible)
Stay focused (your phone will survive)
Actually participate (not just standing there)
Be grateful (better than complaining)
BOSS BATTLE: COMMON OBSTACLES
Level 1: Morning Struggles
Boss: Comfy Bed
Special Move: "Five More Minutes"
Counter: Just roll out immediately
Level 2: Travel Troubles
Boss: Running Late
Special Move: "Maybe Next Week"
Counter: Plan ahead, leave early
Level 3: Focus Failures
Boss: Wandering Mind
Special Move: "So Bored..."
Counter: Actually try to pay attention
FINAL SCORE CHECK
Remember:
Missing Mass without reason = Major Fail
Skipping Communion = Missing Power-Ups
Choosing sleep = Losing Grace
Making excuses = Missing Blessings
YOUR MISSION, SHOULD YOU CHOOSE TO ACCEPT IT:
Show up (physically and mentally)

Pay attention (your phone will wait)
Receive worthily (confession if needed)
Be grateful (attitude matters)
Because sometimes the best drops aren't in your favorite game - they're at the communion rail!

SECRET CHEAT CODE FOR SUCCESS:
Prayer > Excuses
Grace > Games
God > Sleep
Eternity > Temporary Fun
Remember: Jesus showed up for you (died on a cross and everything). You can show up for Him!

END USER AGREEMENT:
Terms: Show up
Conditions: Be prepared
Duration: Forever
Rewards: Out of this world

P.S. - If you think getting up for church is hard, remember Jesus got up from the dead for you! Beat that for motivation! 😊

[Game Save Successful] [Divine Connection Established] [Eternal Rewards Pending...]

Book 4, Chapter 11: The Ultimate Power Duo: Jesus and the Bible!

LOADING ESSENTIAL SURVIVAL GUIDE... [■■■■■■■■■] 100% COMPLETE

THE SUPER SACRED PART (Maximum Respect Required!)

The Most Holy Eucharist and Sacred Scripture are like the ultimate tag team of spiritual power. In the Blessed Sacrament, we receive Jesus Himself - His actual Body, Blood, Soul, and Divinity. Through Scripture, God speaks directly to our hearts. Together, they're like having both the map AND the power-up in the ultimate game of life!

WHY THIS DUO IS BETTER THAN BATMAN AND ROBIN

✹ DYNAMIC DUO COMPARISON CHART ✹

Superheroes	God's Dream Team
Batman & Robin	Scripture & Eucharist
PB & J	Bible & Communion
Mario & Luigi	Word & Sacrament
Sock & Shoe	Reading & Receiving

TOP 10 REASONS WHY YOU NEED BOTH:

Scripture Without Communion is Like:

A phone without a charger
A game without controls
A car without fuel
A lightsaber without power

Communion Without Scripture is Like:

A map you can't read
Powers you don't know how to use
Cheat codes you don't understand
A controller with no instructions

THE EPIC COMBO MOVES

POWER COMBINATION	RESULT
Read + Receive	Maximum Impact
Study + Consume	Ultimate Growth
Learn + Live	Legendary Status

POWER COMBINATION	RESULT
Know + Go	Divine Victory

HOW TO LEVEL UP BOTH SKILLS
Scripture Skills:
Copy
ROOKIE: "Where's Psalms again?"
AMATEUR: "I know some Bible stories!"
PRO: "Let me show you that verse..."
LEGEND: "This applies to life because..."

Communion Game:
Copy
BEGINNER: Shows up sometimes
INTERMEDIATE: Prepares properly
ADVANCED: Understands the gift
MASTER: Lives it daily

SURVIVAL TIPS FOR BOTH
For Scripture:
Don't just use it for random page flips
It's not a fortune cookie book
Actually try to understand it
Yes, the Old Testament counts too

For Communion:
It's not a spiritual drive-through
Actually prepare yourself
Pay attention during Mass
Remember Who you're receiving

COMMON ROOKIE MISTAKES
Scripture Fails:
✖ Using it only to win arguments ✖ Reading one verse per year ✖ Treating it like a magic 8-ball ✖ Never opening it except at church

Communion Fails:
✖ Spiritual sleepwalking ✖ Treating it like routine ✖ Forgetting Who it is ✖ Playing spiritual zombie

THE ULTIMATE POWER-UP STRATEGY
Daily Game Plan:

Morning Scripture Time
Even if it's just one verse
Before checking your phone
Actually think about it
Try to live it
Communion Prep:
Regular confession
Actual preparation
Real participation
True thanksgiving

ACHIEVEMENT UNLOCKED: DUAL MASTERY
Requirements:
Regular Bible reading ✓
Frequent Communion ✓
Actual understanding ✓
Real application ✓

BOSS BATTLES TO WATCH OUT FOR

The Laziness Boss:
Special Attack: "I'll read it later"
Defense: Set a specific time
Counter Move: Just do it now

The Distraction Monster:
Special Attack: Phone notifications
Defense: Airplane mode
Counter Move: Fixed prayer time

YOUR DAILY QUEST LOG:

For Scripture:
Read something (anything!)
Think about it (actually think!)
Try to apply it (yes, really!)
Share what you learned (be cool about it)

For Communion:
Prepare well (confession if needed)
Show up (physically AND mentally)
Receive reverently (it's literally Jesus!)
Thank Him after (don't rush off)

FINAL POWER-UP NOTES

Remember:
These are better than any video game boost
More valuable than rare Pokemon cards
Worth more than your entire game collection
More powerful than any superhero combo
Because sometimes the best strategy guide is the Bible, and the best power-up is Jesus Himself!

SECRET BONUS LEVEL:
When you combine both:
Your spiritual stats max out
Your grace levels overflow
Your resistance to temptation increases
Your eternal high score climbs

P.S. - If you spent as much time on these as you do on video games, you'd probably be a saint by now! But start small - God's cool with level 1 players too! 😇

[SAVE POINT REACHED] [DIVINE WISDOM ACQUIRED] [ETERNAL REWARDS PENDING...]

Remember: This duo is more powerful than any Marvel team-up, and way more useful than your rarest trading cards! Now go forth and power up! 🚀✨

Book 4, Chapter 12: Getting Ready to Meet Jesus: The Ultimate Pre-Game Guide!

[INITIALIZING DIVINE PREPARATION SEQUENCE...] [ACCESSING HOLY WISDOM DATABASE...] [ACTIVATING SUPER-SERIOUS MODE FOR SACRED PARTS...]

THE SACRED STUFF (READ THIS WITH YOUR SERIOUS FACE ON)

Preparing to receive the Most Holy Eucharist is the most important preparation you'll ever make. This isn't like getting ready for a test or preparing for a big game – this is getting ready to receive Jesus Christ Himself, truly present in the Blessed Sacrament. It's a moment where heaven meets earth, where the infinite God becomes our spiritual food.

NOW FOR YOUR PREPARATION WALKTHROUGH

LEVEL 1: THE MIND GAME

Copy

STATUS CHECK:

☐ Brain focused on Jesus

☐ Thoughts cleared of nonsense

☐ Attitude adjusted to 'awesome'

☐ Spiritual antennae activated

LEVEL 2: THE HEART CHECK

Copy

PRE-COMMUNION DIAGNOSTIC:

♥☐ Status: Needs tuning

🎮 Distractions: Too many

📱 Phone addiction: Critical

🙇 Prayer life: Could use a boost

THE "DON'T EVEN THINK ABOUT IT" LIST

Things to Avoid:

Zombie mode walking to communion

Thinking about lunch during Mass

Planning your next video game strategy

Counting ceiling tiles instead of praying

PREPARATION POWER MOVES

Step 1: The Clean-Up Quest

Think of it like cleaning your room, but for your soul:
Under the spiritual bed ✓
Behind the conscience couch ✓
In the closet of bad habits ✓
That one corner where you hide stuff ✓

Step 2: The Focus Challenge
Difficulty Settings:
EASY: Basic prayers
MEDIUM: Actually meaning them
HARD: No distractions
LEGENDARY: Total concentration

THE PRE-COMMUNION CHECKLIST
Physical Prep:
🕐 One hour fast (no, sleep doesn't count) 👕 Decent clothes (superhero PJs are for home) ☐ Basic hygiene (yes, this matters) ☐ Actually arrive on time (a miracle?)

Spiritual Prep:
🙏 Prayer (real ones, not just "God, hi") 🎯 Focus (harder than it sounds) ❤☐ Reverence (like meeting a king, because you are!) 😇 Clean soul (confession if needed)

BOSS BATTLES TO OVERCOME
Boss Level 1: The Sleepy Monster
Special Attack: "Five more minutes"
Weakness: Cold water to the face
Strategy: Just get up!

Boss Level 2: The Distraction Demon
Special Attack: Random thoughts
Weakness: Actual concentration
Strategy: Focus power-ups

Boss Level 3: The Boredom Beast
Special Attack: Mind wandering
Weakness: Real engagement
Strategy: Active participation

ACHIEVEMENT UNLOCKED: PROPER PREP
Requirements for Success:
Copy

SPIRITUAL STATUS:

✓ Soul: Clean

✓ Mind: Focused

✓ Heart: Ready

✓ Attitude: On point

EMERGENCY PROTOCOLS

When Things Go Wrong:

Refocus immediately

Quick prayer boost

Attitude adjustment

Emergency grace request

THE FINAL COUNTDOWN

T-minus preparation sequence:

Night before: Early bed (yes, really)

Morning of: Actual breakfast

Hour before: No snacking

Minutes before: Final prayer check

COMMON PREP FAILS

DO NOT:

Treat it like a drive-through

Show up half asleep

Wing it without preparation

Rush through everything

ULTIMATE SUCCESS STRATEGIES

Remember:

This is bigger than:

Meeting your favorite YouTuber

Getting a new gaming console

Finding a legendary Pokemon

Beating your hardest game

This requires more prep than:

Your biggest test

The hardest game level

Meeting your crush

The school dance

SECRET BONUS TIPS

For Maximum Effect:

Arrive early (shocking, I know)
Actually pray (not just sit there)
Pay attention (your phone will survive)
Be grateful (it's literally Jesus!)

FINAL BOSS WISDOM

Remember:

Jesus is more important than breakfast

Grace beats gaming

Prayer tops Pokemon

Communion beats collecting anything

Because preparing to meet Jesus should be bigger than prepping for:

Your game tournament

Your YouTube channel

Your sports match

Your everything else

P.S. Think about it: Jesus prepared 33 years to give you this gift. You can spend a few minutes preparing to receive it!

[PREPARATION SEQUENCE COMPLETE] [READINESS LEVEL: INCREASING] [GRACE STATUS: DOWNLOADING...]

Now go forth and prepare like you've never prepared before!

Just remember: This is the one prep that literally lasts forever!

✹†☐